GREATEST
RIVALRIES

Written by
Jake Black

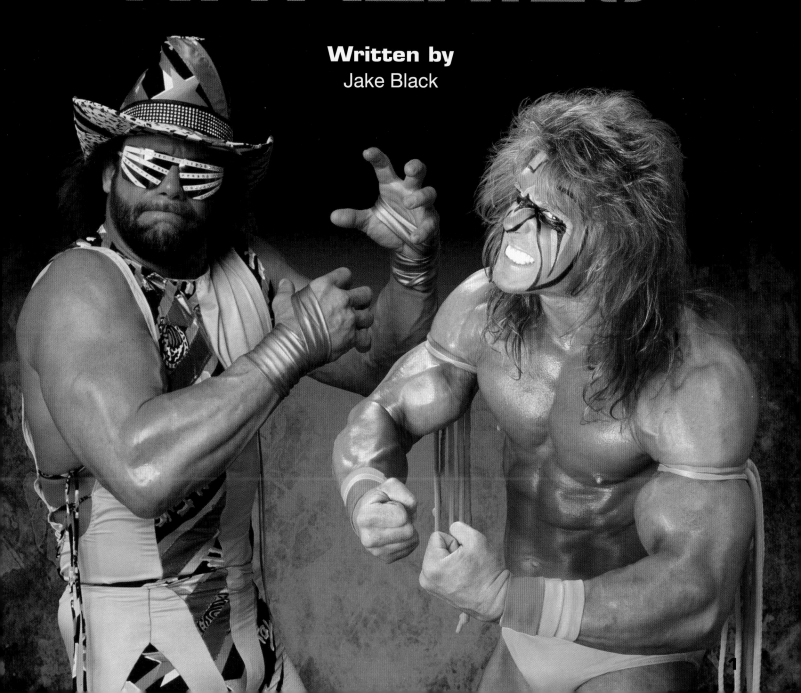

ATTITUDE ERA 7

CLASSIC

ERA

BRUNO SAMMARTINO

VS.

"SUPERSTAR" BILLY GRAHAM

Bruno Sammartino grew up in a poor, tough Italian neighborhood, and fought his way to the WWE Championship with hard work and quiet dignity. "Superstar" Billy Graham was a loud, flashy showman who embodied the counterculture of the 1970s. The two men couldn't have been more different, and that's what made their rivalry so compelling. They battled each other countless times in the 1970s, their clashes becoming the stuff of sports entertainment legend.

1. First match

Boston, November 29, 1975: As a newcomer to WWE, "Superstar" Billy Graham had a lot to prove. He knew he would have to beat the best to show the world that his nickname was justified. Graham faced WWE Champion Bruno Sammartino for the first time in Boston, Massachusetts's legendary arena the Boston Garden, losing the match but gaining a fierce desire to meet Bruno again.

> **"When you get in that ring, it's about how much you have in your heart."**
> —Bruno Sammartino

2. A takedown in Texas

Pittsburgh, April 9, 1976: For months, Sammartino and Graham battled for the WWE Championship without a conclusive winner, their matches ending in draws, countouts, or disqualifications. The Superstars then battled in a Texas Death Match with just one rule—the winner must pin his opponent for a ten count. Using chairs and other objects, Bruno pinned Graham for the count and took the victory.

RIVAL FACTS

- Bruno Sammartino was a two-time WWE Champion, holding the Title longer than anyone before or since. "Superstar" Billy Graham held the WWE Championship once, after beating Sammartino.

- Both Sammartino and Graham are WWE Hall of Famers. Graham was inducted in 2004; Sammartino was inducted in 2013.

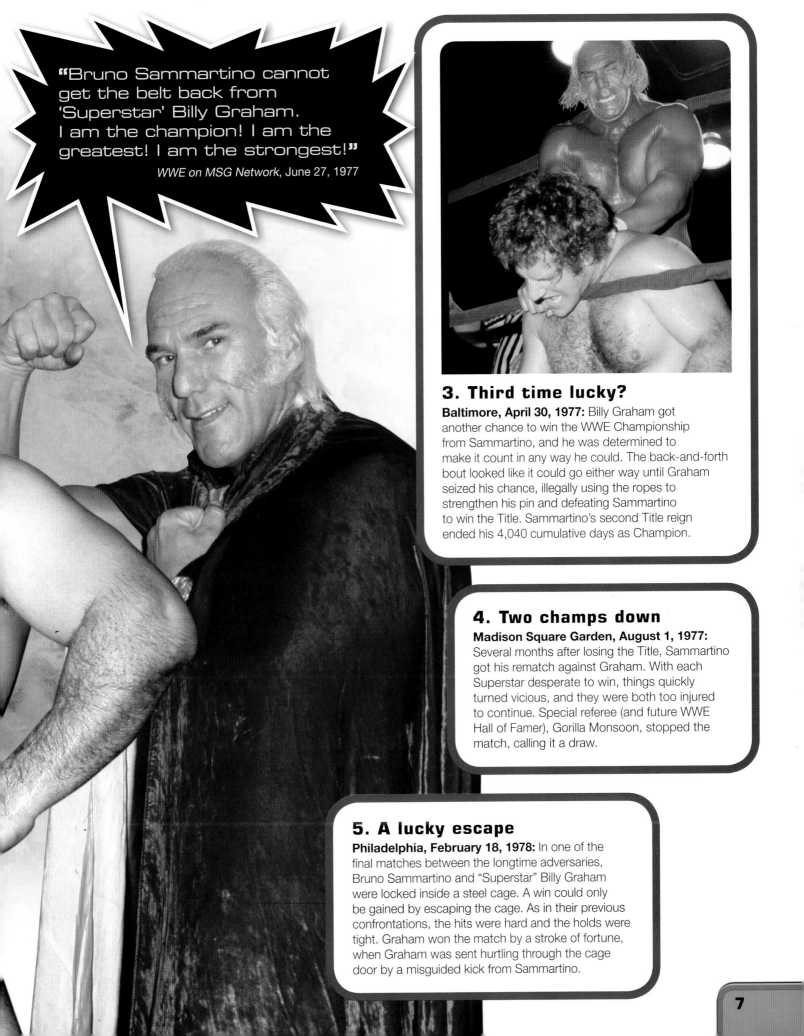

3. Third time lucky?

Baltimore, April 30, 1977: Billy Graham got another chance to win the WWE Championship from Sammartino, and he was determined to make it count in any way he could. The back-and-forth bout looked like it could go either way until Graham seized his chance, illegally using the ropes to strengthen his pin and defeating Sammartino to win the Title. Sammartino's second Title reign ended his 4,040 cumulative days as Champion.

4. Two champs down

Madison Square Garden, August 1, 1977: Several months after losing the Title, Sammartino got his rematch against Graham. With each Superstar desperate to win, things quickly turned vicious, and they were both too injured to continue. Special referee (and future WWE Hall of Famer), Gorilla Monsoon, stopped the match, calling it a draw.

5. A lucky escape

Philadelphia, February 18, 1978: In one of the final matches between the longtime adversaries, Bruno Sammartino and "Superstar" Billy Graham were locked inside a steel cage. A win could only be gained by escaping the cage. As in their previous confrontations, the hits were hard and the holds were tight. Graham won the match by a stroke of fortune, when Graham was sent hurtling through the cage door by a misguided kick from Sammartino.

ANDRÉ THE GIANT
VS.
HULK HOGAN

For three years, support had been strong for WWE Champion Hulk Hogan among the fans he called "Hulkmaniacs." André the Giant had always been in the background quietly supporting his friend Hogan. But André became jealous and wanted a Championship Match. André's determination soon made him the immovable object with which Hogan would collide.

7ft 4in (2.25m)

> **"You think I taught you everything you know in professional wrestling? Believe me, I didn't."**
>
> *Wrestling Challenge*, February 27, 1987

1. Challenged
***Superstars*, February 7, 1987:** André interrupted Hogan during an interview on the Piper's Pit talk show. André introduced his new manager Bobby "The Brain" Heenan and demanded a WWE Championship Match at *WrestleMania III*. Hogan begged André to reconsider, as he didn't want to fight his friend. André grew angry and ripped off Hogan's shirt and beloved crucifix necklace, setting the pair on a path to conflict.

2. Record-breaking moment
***WrestleMania III*, March 29, 1987:** 93,000 fans broke the world record for largest indoor crowd when they gathered to watch Hogan and André at *WrestleMania III*. Hogan initially struggled when his rival was able to use his size advantage to squeeze Hogan with a bear hug. However, the Champion ultimately produced a spectacular feat of strength, bodyslamming André to the mat and successfully defending his Title.

RIVAL FACTS

● André the Giant and Hulk Hogan were both inducted into the WWE Hall of Fame—André in 1993, Hogan more than a decade later in 2005.

● André's victory over Hogan was his only reign as WWE Champion. Hulk Hogan is recognized as a 12-time World Heavyweight Champion.

● Both Hogan and André are one-time WWE Tag Team Champions.

3. Title rematch

The Main Event, February 5, 1988: André the Giant was granted another opportunity at Hogan's WWE Championship, this time with "Million Dollar Man" Ted DiBiase and DiBiase's assistant Virgil in his corner. DiBiase and Virgil distracted the referee when Hogan had André pinned. André got out of the pin and threw Hogan to the mat, pinning him for three, and finally winning the WWE Championship.

> "Fee fie foe fum, your time has come, André!"
>
> *WrestleMania IV,* March 27, 1988

6ft 7in (2.01m)

4. Up for grabs

WrestleMania IV, March 27, 1988: Immediately after winning the WWE Championship, André the Giant gave it to Ted DiBiase, in return for an enormous sum of money. This contravened WWE rules, so André was stripped of the Title and a tournament was held at *WrestleMania IV* to crown a new Champion. Hogan and André battled in the first round of the tournament. Both Hogan and André hit each other with steel chairs early in the match, resulting in a double disqualification and the elimination of both men from the tournament.

5. Into the cage

WrestleFest, July 31, 1988: There was only one way for these former friends to settle their differences—inside a steel cage. Both Hogan and André struck some mighty blows before André's manager Bobby Heenan entered the cage and hit Hogan with brass knuckles. This bought André some time to climb the cage, but Hogan swiftly dealt with Heenan and tied André up in the ropes. With André incapacitated, Hogan climbed out of the cage for the win.

BEFORE WRESTLEMANIA

Hogan and André had several matches against each other, years before their epic *WrestleMania III* match.

Binghamton, New York (March 28, 1980) The first match between Hogan and André resulted in a double countout draw when both Superstars fought outside the ring.

WWE on PRISM Network (July 26, 1980) André the Giant defeated Hogan in their first televised match, broadcast from the Philadelphia Spectrum.

Showdown at Shea (August 9, 1980) At an event held at the home of baseball team the New York Mets, Shea Stadium, André won by pinfall, after which Hogan hit him with brass knuckles provided by his manager "Classy" Freddie Blassie.

WWE on MSG Network (September 22, 1980) André the Giant once again defeated Hulk Hogan, this time when special guest referee Gorilla Monsoon counted the three.

DON MURACO
VS.
JIMMY "SUPERFLY" SNUKA

Don Muraco and Jimmy "Superfly" Snuka were both very proud men. They both felt they'd earned the respect of their peers in WWE, and were very angry if they felt disrespected. This level of personal pride caused these two Superstars to butt heads as they demanded more respect from each other. Throw the Intercontinental Championship in the mix, and they had the formula for an exciting and legendary rivalry.

DID YOU KNOW?
Don Muraco and Jimmy Snuka competed in the ring against each for the ECW Championship.

"Jimmy Snuka, as much as they love you, they love to hate me. Because when I'm bad, I'm so good!"
WWE Championship Wrestling, July 2, 1983

1. Disrespected
WWE Championship Wrestling, June 18, 1983:
Don Muraco was seated for an interview on the Roger's Corner talk show segment when Snuka came to the ring, interrupting the interview. Highly insulted, Muraco went to the ring and spat at Snuka. Snuka responded by diving out of the ring onto Muraco, and began ripping Muraco's clothes off, until several Superstars came from the back of the auditorium to stop his attack.

2. Who's the Champ?

WWE on PRISM Network,
July 16, 1983: Muraco had made his
name by winning the Intercontinental
Championship. Snuka wanted that Title
and a rematch with Muraco following
their encounter a month earlier. With
former WWE Champion "Nature Boy"
Buddy Rogers in his corner, Snuka
made a valiant effort to win the
Championship but lost his head and
was disqualified for hitting the referee.

3. A special referee

WWE on PRISM Network, **August 13, 1983:**
Snuka was granted another opportunity
to capture Muraco's Intercontinental
Championship. To ensure the referee wouldn't
be pushed around this time, Superstar Swede
Hanson served as a special guest referee.
Snuka won the bout, but not the Title, as
Muraco left the ring and didn't return before
referee Hanson had finished his count.

4. Cage flight

WWE on MSG Network, **October 17, 1983:**
This was arguably the most famous cage match
in WWE history, but not because of the match
itself, which Muraco won, retaining his
Championship. However, what happened after
the match was truly shocking. Snuka dragged
Muraco back inside the steel structure, climbed
to the top of the cage, and dove more than 15ft
(4.6m), crashing onto Muraco and giving the
WWE Universe a moment they'd never forget.

> **"I'm going to give
> my all out there,
> Don Muraco.
> You have brought
> out the animal in
> me because of
> what you did.
> Believe that!"**
>
> *WWE on MSG Network,*
> October 17, 1983

RIVAL FACTS

- Snuka and Muraco were both inducted
into the WWE Hall of Fame. Snuka was
inducted by Don Muraco in 1996. Muraco
was inducted by Mick Foley in 2004.

- Don Muraco was a two-time
Intercontinental Champion and a
former King of the Ring.

5. Fijian Strap Match

WWE on PRISM Network, **October 22, 1983:**
After steel cages, special referees, and ringside
attacks, Snuka and Muraco had one more match for
the Intercontinental Championship. This time it was
a Fijian Strap Match, where the Superstars were tied
together by a leather strap. Muraco took the strap off
and whipped Snuka with it, getting himself disqualified
and losing the match, but not the Championship.

BRUNO SAMMARTINO
VS.
LARRY ZBYSZKO

In 1973, Larry Zbyszko was a big Bruno Sammartino fan. So big, in fact, that he was inspired to drop out of college and begin training for sports entertainment in a bid to be like his idol. Larry knew that to be a Superstar he had to learn from the best, so he sought out his hero and begged him to be his mentor. Initially uninterested, Bruno was won over by Zbyszko's persistence, and finally agreed to train him for in-ring competition. All went fine—until the day Zbyszko decided to come out of Sammartino's shadow.

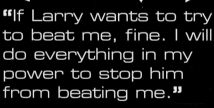

THE BREAKUP

"If Larry wants to try to beat me, fine. I will do everything in my power to stop him from beating me."
Championship Wrestling, January 26, 1980

1. From the shadows
Zbyszko became a Tag Team Champion, and his popularity grew. With his career in sports entertainment taking off, he felt it was time to really prove himself. What better way than by beating his own mentor, Bruno Sammartino? At first, Bruno refused the match, but finally accepted, promising he wouldn't beat up his own student but Zbyszko would have to beat him.

2. Student vs. teacher
Wrestling Challenge, **February 2, 1980:**
The appointed day came, and Larry Zbyszko finally got his chance to compete against his teacher. Sammartino appeared to be the superior competitor, but honoring his decision not to beat up his student, he immediately released any holds he applied. Infuriated, Zbyszko grabbed a ringside chair and pummeled Sammartino with it, leaving his mentor severely injured.

3. Continued clashes

Summer 1980: In the months that followed, Sammartino and Zbyszko faced each other in the ring several times, but there was never a clear-cut winner. The matches usually ended in draws or disqualifications when one of the Superstars used weapons to punish the other. With the rivalry growing more intense and more ferocious, WWE officials realized there was only one way to finish it—inside a steel cage.

> **"I want Bruno to come out here and say to my face if he'll wrestle me!"**
>
> *Championship Wrestling*, January 26, 1980

4. The final lesson?

***Showdown at Shea,* August 9, 1980:** Held in New York City's Shea Stadium, it was one of the biggest events WWE had ever produced—*Showdown at Shea*. This time, Sammartino did not release any holds. He wanted to teach his former student a lesson he wouldn't forget—that he, Bruno Sammartino, was still the master. After punishing Zbyszko for nearly 20 minutes, Sammartino escaped the cage to win the match.

DID YOU KNOW?
Following their retirements, Sammartino and Zbyszko both became commentators.

THE MAKEUP

5. Mutual respect

After Sammartino exited the cage at Shea Stadium, Zbyszko followed him out. Thinking that Zybszko wanted to carry on the fight, Sammartino hit him one more time. But fighting wasn't on Zybszko's mind. Shrugging off the hit, he raised Sammartino's hand in a grudging show of respect. A short time later, Zbyszko left WWE, and Sammartino announced his formal retirement.

ANDRÉ THE GIANT

VS.

BIG JOHN STUDD

520lbs (235.90kg)

André the Giant was known throughout his career as the number one giant in sports entertainment. But when a newcomer to WWE named Big John Studd arrived on the scene, he tried to take away André's claim. André was furious and fought Studd countless times. When these two behemoths collided, it was almost as if the earth itself shook.

> "John Studd, you want to be the giant, you have to defeat The Giant."
>
> *WWE on MSG Network, July 30, 1983*

DID YOU KNOW?

André was the very first inductee into the WWE Hall of Fame in 1993. Studd was inducted in 2004.

1. Bodyslam survivor

WWE Championship Wrestling,
February 26, 1983: Each week, Studd held an open "Bodyslam Challenge," where Superstars tried to win an ever-growing pot of money if they could bodyslam Studd. Studd thought the Superstar challenging that week was Chief Jay Strongbow, but it was revealed to be the mammoth André the Giant. As André was about to slam Studd, Studd's manager Classy Freddy Blassie stopped him, saving Studd and the money.

2. Battle of the giants

Boston Garden, March 18, 1983: Following the bodyslam challenge the previous month, André met Studd one-on-one in a WWE ring for the first time at the historic Boston Garden arena. André used his bigger size to his advantage, giving Studd a bearhug that forced the smaller giant to submit. Humiliated, Studd vowed to get even with André at a future meeting.

"I am the true giant of professional wrestling, André!"

WWE on MSG Network, July 23, 1983

364lbs (165kg)

3. Tempers flare

WWE on USA Network, **April 23, 1983:** Studd had another chance to battle André and prove his dominance. This time, the two giants completely lost their tempers. They grabbed chairs and attacked each other with them. The referee disqualified them both, making the match a draw.

CAGE MATCHES

André the Giant and Big John Studd's rivalry was so intense, they tried to settle it while contained inside a steel cage.

Boston Garden (June 11, 1983) André defeated Big John Studd for the victory in their first cage match.

Medowlands in New Jersey (July 11, 1983) André escaped the cage for the win.

WWE on MSG Network (July 30, 1983) André the Giant jumped off the top rope, sitting on Studd and then walking out of the cage to win.

WWE on PRISM Network (September 24, 1983) Once again, André overpowered Big John Studd, allowing him to escape the cage and win the match.

4. André's haircut

WWE Championship Wrestling, **November 13, 1984:** Studd teamed with Ken Patera to face André and SD Jones. Both teams violated the referee's instructions, resulting in a double disqualification. After the match, Patera and Studd then humiliated André by cutting his long hair while he lay helpless in the ring.

RIVAL FACTS

● Both giants were one-time WWE Tag Team Champions.

● André briefly held the WWE Championship, while Studd never won that Title.

● Big John Studd won the 1989 Royal Rumble Match, defeating 29 other Superstars, including André the Giant.

5. Slamming Studd

WrestleMania, **March 31, 1985:** Just as they had years earlier, André and Studd competed in a Bodyslam Challenge. This time, Studd bet $15,000 André couldn't slam him. André said he would retire if he couldn't slam Studd on the grandest stage of all: the first *WrestleMania*. André not only slammed Studd, he threw his prize money into the stands, sharing it with the WWE Universe.

JIMMY "SUPERFLY" SNUKA

VS.

"ROWDY" RODDY PIPER

"Rowdy" Roddy Piper hadn't been in WWE very long before he started making his fellow Superstars and the WWE Universe extremely angry with him. Using his Piper's Pit talk show segment as his personal platform, Piper insulted everyone and anyone, with scant regard for reputations or repercussions. Perhaps no WWE Superstar was the target of so many of Piper's barbs as "Superfly" Jimmy Snuka—stoking a series of memorably extreme encounters.

THE BREAKUP

1. First time in the pit

"Rowdy" Roddy Piper invited Jimmy "Superfly" Snuka to be his guest on the Piper's Pit talk show on March 24, 1984 and June 26, 1984. True to form, Piper asked Snuka several insulting questions and was condescending on Snuka's first appearance. On his second appearance, Piper behaved even more viciously. He pretended to apologize to Snuka, and then pelted him with fruit instead. Snuka finally snapped and tried to get back at Piper, but Piper ran away.

2. Fight!

WWE on PRISM, **March 17, 1985:** A couple of weeks after their second brawl on Piper's Pit, Snuka and Piper met again in the ring. Snuka was out for revenge, Piper responded, and they attacked each other mercilessly. Piper tried to escape the ring, but Snuka flew from the top rope, landing on Piper. Piper got back in the ring just before the referee's count finished. Snuka lost by a countout, but gave Piper quite a beating.

3. Out of time

WWE on MSG Network, **July 15, 1984:** Piper and Snuka had their final one-on-one fight one week before the first-ever *WrestleMania,* where Snuka would be in the corner of Piper's opponents Hulk Hogan and Mr. T. The tension between the two Superstars was palpable, with them fighting hard in and out of the ring. This time, their out-of-the-ring brawl resulted in both men being counted out.

4. Old wounds

SmackDown, **April 19, 2003:** Nearly two decades after his first appearance on Piper's Pit, Snuka was invited back on the show. Neither Piper nor Snuka was ready to set past differences aside. The interview turned into yet another brawl. Piper's protegé, Sean O'Haire, helped attack Snuka, who was saved when his nephew Rikishi hit the ring and fought off O'Haire and Piper.

> **"**People tell me I beat Jimmy Snuka within an inch of his life. Silly me. Next time I'll go an inch further.**"**
>
> *Boston Garden,* June 30, 1984

THE MAKEUP

5. The enemy of my ene

As *WrestleMania XXV* was approachir began targeting WWE Hall of Famers insulting them and discrediting their le attacked Piper and Snuka, as well as Flair and Ricky "The Dragon" Steambe Piper decided to set aside their decac and team up against Jericho in a Han

IRON SHEIK

VS.

SGT. SLAUGHTER

DID YOU KNOW?
More than 15 years after their rivalry ended, Slaughter and Sheik renewed their enmity. They were the last men standing in the Battle Royal Match at *WrestleMania X-Seven*.

Sgt. Slaughter claimed to be a proud patriot. The former U.S. Marine Drill Sergeant professed to love America and was determined to defend it against all potential enemies. The Iron Sheik was just as proud of his nation, Iran, and had competed in the Olympics on behalf of the country. These two bitter rivals clashed over which was the greatest country— the U.S. or Iran.

"Iran number one!"
WWE on PRISM Network,
November 10, 1984

1. Pride

WWE Championship Wrestling, February 18, 1984: Sgt. Slaughter and Iron Sheik both came to the ring waving the flags of their respective countries. Before the match could even begin, the Sheik attacked Slaughter from behind. Sheik continued his assault using a leather belt to whip Slaughter. Sheik escaped the ring before Slaughter could fight back, and Slaughter swore revenge.

2. It's nonstop war!

WWE on MSG Network, April 23, 1984: This match was so intense, the announcers even referred to it as "World War III." The Iron Sheik and Sgt. Slaughter beat on each other with reckless abandon. When Sgt. Slaughter removed his steel-toed combat boot to use as a weapon, he was disqualified. Nevertheless, Sgt. Slaughter and Iron Sheik continued fighting back in the locker room. Superstars and officials had to pull them apart.

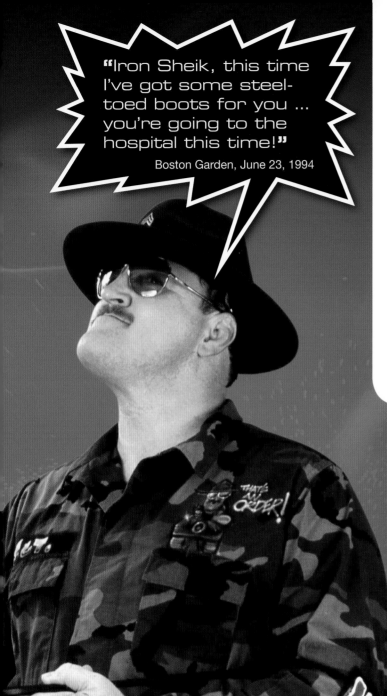

"Iron Sheik, this time I've got some steel-toed boots for you ... you're going to the hospital this time!"

Boston Garden, June 23, 1994

3. Anger

WWE on USA Network, May 19, 1984: The Iron Sheik entered the ring holding a picture of the Iranian leader. Sgt. Slaughter arrived waving the American flag. Once again their match became very violent. Iron Sheik drove his pointed-toe boots at Slaughter. Slaughter worked to remove the boot and use it on Sheik. Several Superstars tried to stop Slaughter using the boot, and the referee declared the match a double-disqualification draw.

4. Four-way battle

WWE on PRISM Network, November 10, 1984: Iron Sheik had recruited the Soviet Union's Nikolai Volkoff, forming a tag team. They targeted Sgt. Slaughter for a two-on-one attack, but Slaughter found a partner of his own—Junkyard Dog. All four Superstars brawled in the ring at the same time. Sgt. Slaughter caught Iron Sheik in his Cobra Clutch move, knocking him out for the win.

RIVAL FACTS

● Both Sgt. Slaughter and Iron Sheik were one-time WWE Champions.

● Iron Sheik held the Tag Team Championships with Nikolai Volkoff; Sgt. Slaughter never won that Title.

● Both Sgt. Slaughter (2004) and Iron Sheik (2005) were inducted into the WWE Hall of Fame. In fact, Sgt. Slaughter inducted Sheik into the Hall of Fame himself!

BOOT CAMP MATCHES

With tempers so hot and action so violent, Sgt. Slaughter and Iron Sheik set aside the rules to battle each other in Boot Camp Matches, where weapons, interference, and more could be used. Here are their best Boot Camp Matches.

WWE on USA Network (June 9, 1984) Sgt. Slaughter defeated Iron Sheik in their first Boot Camp encounter.

WWE on MSG Network (June 16, 1984) Slaughter legally used Iron Sheik's boot against him to get the win.

Pittsburgh, Pennsylvania (June 22, 1984) Sgt. Slaughter again outlasted Iron Sheik.

San Diego, California (November 23, 1984) In their final Boot Camp Match, Sgt. Slaughter defeated the Iron Sheik, seemingly putting an end to their rivalry.

5. No real winner

WWE on MSG Network, March 17, 1985: This battle between Sgt. Slaughter and Sheik escalated dramatically when Iron Sheik began using every weapon he could lay his hands on. He hit Slaughter with chairs, rammed him into the steel ring post and stairs, and even used the sharp points on his boots. Sgt. Slaughter was clearly hurt, but fought through the pain to battle Iron Sheik, until the referee stopped the match, and declared it a double-disqualification draw.

LEILANI KAI
VS.
WENDI RICHTER

Wendi Richter and Leilani Kai were the top female Superstars of the 1980s. Their colorful in-ring gear reflected the fun-focused lifestyle of the time, but their mutual hatred was a serious matter. The two women first became rivals because of issues between their managers, The Fabulous Moolah for Kai, and rock star Cyndi Lauper for Richter. It wasn't long before they began a war of their own, trading victories, titles... and more than a few insults.

> "I don't care what I got to do or how I got to do it to beat Wendi, I'm gonna do it."
>
> *WrestleMania*, March 31, 1985

1. Piper's Pit

Championship Wrestling, **June 16, 1984:** WWE Hall of Fame Manager Captain Lou Albano appeared in Cyndi Lauper's music video "Girls Just Want to Have Fun" and began to take credit for Lauper's success. This angered Lauper, so when Lauper appeared on the Piper's Pit talk show segment to counter Albano's claims, she challenged one of his Superstars to a match against a Superstar of her choice.

2. Winner takes all

MTV's Brawl To End It All, **July 23, 1984:** Albano chose WWE Women's Champion The Fabulous Moolah as his Superstar. Lauper chose her friend, Wendi Richter. The televised match ended with Moolah rolling up Richter, thinking she'd pinned her opponent. However, it was her own, not Richter's shoulders, that were both down. Richter was the new Champion. As Lauper celebrated, the bad blood between herself and Moolah began to bubble.

3. A younger challenger

MTV's War to Settle the Score,
February 18, 1985: Wounded by the loss, Moolah plotted her revenge. Thinking a younger challenger would stand more of a chance against Richter, she found Leilani Kai. This young, strong Superstar was both ambitious and ruthless. Kai and Richter had an intense battle for the Championship, but Moolah interfered with the match, helping Kai win. Lauper protested, but it wasn't about managers anymore. Richter had taken Kai's cheating personally.

> **"Leilani Kai, girls just want to have fun, and I'm going to have fun with you, taking my Title back."**
>
> *WWE All American Wrestling,* March 10, 1985

4. Rematch

Maple Leaf Gardens, **March 10, 1985:** Richter had an unsuccessful rematch against Kai for the Women's Championship in Toronto, Canada. Neither Superstar had her manager with her, but Kai was able to capitalize on a small technical mistake from Richter and squeak out a win. Richter was not discouraged. She knew she would have her chance at the inaugural *WrestleMania* just a few weeks later.

DID YOU KNOW?
When Wendi Richter won the WWE Women's Championship from The Fabulous Moolah, it ended Moolah's 28-year Title reign, the longest of any Championship in WWE history.

5. Revenge at last

WrestleMania, **March 31, 1985:** With Lauper in her corner once again, Richter had another opportunity to win back her WWE Women's Championship. But the Champion, Kai, had Moolah in her corner. This time, Lauper kept Moolah at bay, while Richter defeated Kai to become the first two-time WWE Women's Champion. Richter and Lauper danced for joy after the match.

BRITISH BULLDOGS
VS.
HART FOUNDATION

WWE Hall of Famer Stu Hart trained countless Superstars, including his son Bret "Hit Man" Hart and son-in-law Jim "The Anvil" Neidhart. Another son-in-law, Davey Boy Smith, and Smith's cousin The Dynamite Kid were also trained at Stu's gym called "The Dungeon." The "Hit Man" and "The Anvil" formed a tag team called the Hart Foundation. Dynamite and Davey formed the British Bulldogs. Both teams joined WWE, seeking the WWE Tag Team Championship.

> "Hart Foundation, we're going to go in that ring, and we're going to show no mercy."
>
> —Davey Boy Smith, *Boston Garden*, April 18, 1987

1. On the big stage

***WWE on PRISM Network*, April 27, 1985:** The Hart Foundation and the British Bulldogs had faced each other in Stu Hart's Canadian promotion Stampede Wrestling, but their first chance to show the world on a large scale what they could do was on WWE. Their first match ended in a time-limit draw.

2. Nontitle match

***Superstars*, November 29, 1986:** The British Bulldogs had won the WWE Tag Team Championship at *WrestleMania 2*. The Hart Foundation wanted the Bulldogs' Championship. To prove their worth, the Hart Foundation competed against the Bulldogs in a non-title match. The Hart Foundation won and would get a title match in the coming weeks.

DID YOU KNOW?

The British Bulldogs had a bulldog mascot named Matilda who liked to chase and bite Hart Foundation manager Jimmy Hart.

"The British Chihuahuas … They won't be a problem."

—Jim "The Anvil" Neidhart, *Championship Wrestling,* February 2, 1985

3. Sharp practice

Superstars, **January 26, 1987:** The Hart Foundation used every means at their disposal to win their Championship Match against the British Bulldogs. The Hart Foundation capitalized on their friendship with referee Danny Davis; not only did he ignore cheating by the Harts, he hit a fast count when Bret pinned Davey Boy Smith, enabling the Hart Foundation to become the WWE Tag Team Champions.

4. Six-man tag

WrestleMania III, **March 29, 1987:** Seeking revenge, the British Bulldogs joined with Tito Santana to face the Hart Foundation and their crooked referee friend Danny Davis in a six-man tag team match. The Bulldogs took revenge on Danny Davis, repeatedly hitting and kicking him, but Davis and the Hart Foundation won the match when Davis hit Davey Boy Smith with Jimmy Hart's megaphone.

5. Two out of three

Saturday Night's Main Event, 1987: The Hart Foundation defer their Tag Team Championship a the British Bulldogs in a Two O Three Falls Match. The Bulldo Tito Santana in their corner, Hart Foundation had Danny and Jimmy Hart backing th The British Bulldogs won th with two straight falls; howe because the first fall was the a disqualification, they were n the WWE Tag Team Champion

MR. T

VS.

"ROWDY" RODDY PIPER

Mr. T was a Hollywood star who featured in the mega-popular television series *The A-Team* and the *Rocky* movie franchise. His friendship with Hulk Hogan brought him into the world of sports entertainment. "Rowdy" Roddy Piper considered Mr. T an unwelcome intruder. Over the course of two years and two *WrestleMania* events, Piper and Mr. T came to blows time and time again.

"Roddy Piper, you ain't nothing, man."

Championship Wrestling,
February 16, 1985

1. Mr. T in the ring

***War to Settle the Score*, February 18, 1985:** In a first-of-its-kind television special, *War to Settle the Score* aired on MTV and featured Hulk Hogan defending the WWE Championship against "Rowdy" Roddy Piper. After the match ended in a disqualification victory for Hogan, Mr. T entered the ring to celebrate with his friend. Piper and his friend Paul Orndorff turned on Mr. T, bringing him rapidly into the world of WWE rivalries.

2. Trash talking

***Saturday Night Live*, March 30, 1985:** After Mr. T's abrupt introduction to WWE, he and Hogan challenged Piper and Orndorff to a match at the first *WrestleMania*. Hogan and Mr. T were seen all over the United States training and trash talking about their opponents—even while hosting *Saturday Night Live* the night before the match.

3. The Big One

WrestleMania, March 31, 1985: In the main event of the first *WrestleMania*, Mr. T and Hulk Hogan faced "Rowdy" Roddy Piper and "Mr. Wonderful" Paul Orndorff. The match started with Mr. T and Piper exchanging blows and ended when Piper's friend Bob Orton accidentally knocked out Orndorff, leaving Mr. T and Hogan celebrating their victory.

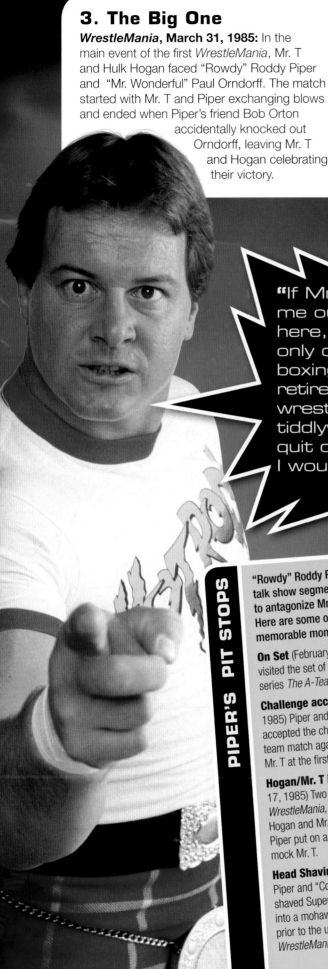

"If Mr. T can knock me out in this fight here, I would not only quit professional boxing, I would quit, retire from professional wrestling, I would quit tiddlywinks, I would quit dating girls. I would quit it all."

WrestleMania 2, April 7, 1986

4. A new challenger

***Saturday Night's Main Event*, March 1, 1986:** Nearly a year later, Piper's friend "Cowboy" Bob Orton issued an open challenge to a boxing match. One of Mr. T's most famous roles had been as a boxer in the 1982 film *Rocky III,* and he readily accepted Orton's challenge. Mr. T won the fight, but afterward Piper and Orton attacked Mr. T. A livid Mr. T then challenged Piper to a boxing match of their own.

PIPER'S PIT STOPS

"Rowdy" Roddy Piper used his talk show segment Piper's Pit to antagonize Mr. T repeatedly. Here are some of the most memorable moments.

On Set (February 16, 1985) Piper visited the set of Mr. T's television series *The A-Team* to insult him.

Challenge accepted (March 2, 1985) Piper and Paul Orndorff accepted the challenge for a tag team match against Hogan and Mr. T at the first *WrestleMania.*

Hogan/Mr. T in the Pit (March 17, 1985) Two weeks before *WrestleMania,* Piper interviewed Hogan and Mr. T in Piper's Pit. Piper put on a mohawk wig to mock Mr. T.

Head Shaving (March 6, 1986) Piper and "Cowboy" Bob Orton shaved Superstar Haiti Kid's head into a mohawk, mocking Mr. T prior to the upcoming *WrestleMania 2* boxing match.

5. Back to box

***WrestleMania 2*, April 7, 1986:** Mr. T and Piper's boxing match became one of the main events at *WrestleMania 2*. The fight started clean, but by the third round, Piper had had enough and bodyslammed Mr. T, getting disqualified in the process. The two continued to brawl for several more minutes until WWE officials pulled them apart.

"MACHO MAN" RANDY SAVAGE

VS.

RICKY "THE DRAGON" STEAMBOAT

Ricky "The Dragon" Steamboat was one of the most talented competitors to ever set foot inside a WWE ring. But more than that, he was a noble family man who always chose the righteous path. Randy "Macho Man" Savage was also extremely talented in the ring, but he didn't have a problem with cutting corners in a match or breaking the rules. The fact Steamboat refused to use underhanded tactics bothered Savage.

"I am the Intercontinental Champion, and I will be after WrestleMania III!"

Prime Time Wrestling,
March 23, 1987

DID YOU KNOW?

The Randy Savage and Ricky Steamboat match at *WrestleMania III* is frequently voted one of the greatest matches of all time by the WWE Universe.

1. Ringing the bell

Superstars, **November 22, 1986:** Savage and Steamboat were engaged in a match when Savage suddenly snapped and became aggressive against his straight-laced opponent. In an attempt to show Steamboat that an underhanded attack is often most effective, he beat up Steamboat, leaving him lying unconscious in the ring. Savage drove home the point by grabbing the timekeeper's bell, before diving off the top rope, slamming the bell into Steamboat.

2. Outrage and updates

Superstars, **November 29, 1986:** There was outrage in WWE at Savage's brutal attack a week earlier, but Savage was proud of his actions. Several Superstars tried attacking Savage in retaliation, but Savage came away unscathed. Then Steamboat's wife Bonnie called into WWE with news on Steamboat's condition—he'd suffered a crushed larynx.

3. Learning to talk again

Superstars, December 20, 1986:
The damage to Steamboat's larynx was so severe he had to relearn how to talk. At the advice of his doctors, Steamboat met with a speech therapist on *Superstars*. As Steamboat struggled to speak, it became clear that Savage would have to be stopped.

RIVAL FACTS

- Ricky Steamboat and Randy Savage were both one-time Intercontinental Champions.
- Randy Savage was the World Heavyweight Champion six times; Ricky Steamboat held the World Heavyweight Championship once. Both Superstars defeated Ric Flair for the World Championship.
- Ricky Steamboat was inducted in 2009; Randy Savage entered the WWE Hall of Fame in 2015.

4. The Dragon returns!

Saturday Night's Main Event, January 3, 1987:
Savage defended his Intercontinental Championship against George "The Animal" Steele. As Steele gained the advantage, Savage grabbed the ringside bell and hit Steele with it to get a pin. After winning the match, Savage attempted to drive the bell into Steele's throat. Not wanting another Superstar to suffer the way he had, a fully recovered Steamboat made a dramatic return to the ring and chased Savage away.

"Randy Savage, this dragon breathes fire and will scorch your back. I will walk away the winner!"

WrestleMania III, March 29, 1987

5. Revenge at *WrestleMania*

WrestleMania III, March 29, 1987:
Steamboat finally got his opportunity for revenge at *WrestleMania III,* as well as a shot at the Intercontinental Championship. The match was a showcase of each Superstar's exceptional ability. After an epic battle, Steamboat finally came out on top and pinned Savage to win the Intercontinental Championship in dramatic style.

HULK HOGAN'S RIVALRIES

In the 1980s, there was no bigger name in WWE than Hulk Hogan. He was so popular, he created a sports entertainment movement called "Hulkamania." Winning the WWE Championship in January 1984 made him a target. Hogan relied on his "Hulkamaniacs" to give him the moral support he needed to overcome a whole host of rivals.

DID YOU KNOW?

Hulk Hogan, Randy "Macho Man" Savage, and Ultimate Warrior are all former WWE Champions, with Hogan having won the most World Titles at 12.

"Rowdy" Roddy Piper

In 1985, "Rowdy" Roddy Piper was jealous of Hogan's popularity and sought to put an end to it. At an event called *War to Settle the Score*, Piper battled Hogan for his WWE Championship. The match ended in a disqualification when Piper's friend Paul Orndorff interfered and attacked Hogan. A main event match at the first *WrestleMania* followed, where Hogan teamed up with Mr. T to defeat Piper and Orndorff. Months later, Piper and Hogan had a rematch for the WWE Championship. Once again, Piper was disqualified after his friend Bob Orton attacked Hogan.

Hogan and Piper didn't face each other again in a one-on-one WWE match until 2003. Hogan, disguised as a masked character named "Mr. America," defeated Piper at the *Judgment Day* pay-per-view in their final confrontation.

"Mr. Wonderful" Paul Orndorff

Early in his WWE career, "Mr. Wonderful" Paul Orndorff had disliked Hulk Hogan, mainly due to his friend "Rowdy" Roddy Piper. However, when Orndorff and Piper's friendship crumbled, Orndorff saved Hogan from several of Piper's sneak attacks. Orndorff now saw Hogan as a mentor and followed him everywhere. It was only when Adrian Adonis made fun of Orndorff for this, that Orndorff changed his tune again. He mocked Hogan and challenged him to a WWE Championship match.

Hogan defeated Orndorff by disqualification when his rival hit the referee. In order to declare a clear-cut winner between them, Orndorff and Hogan had one final match in a steel cage at the January 3, 1987 edition of *Saturday Night's Main Event*, which Hogan won.

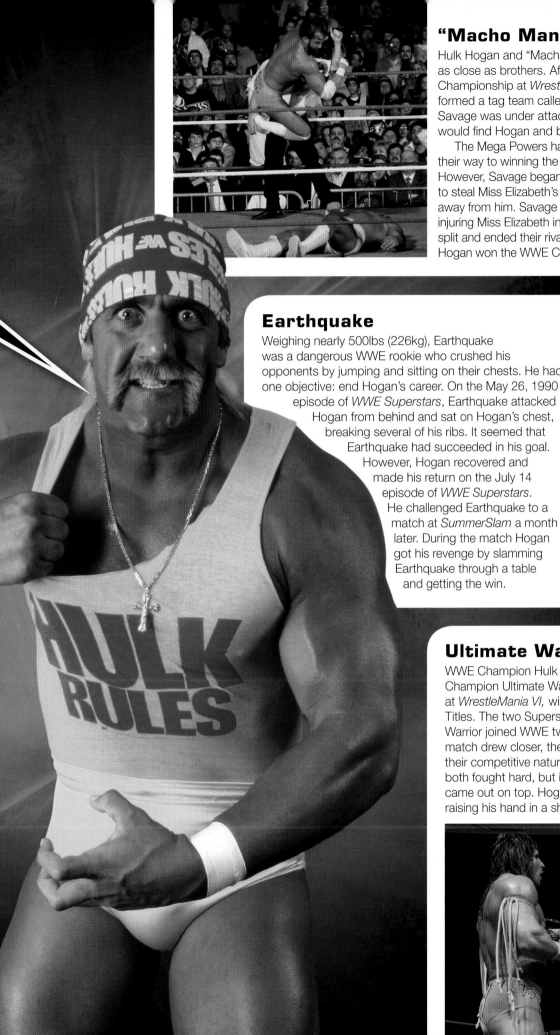

"Macho Man" Randy Savage

Hulk Hogan and "Macho Man" Randy Savage were as close as brothers. After Savage won the WWE Championship at *WrestleMania IV*, he and Hogan formed a tag team called the Mega Powers. Whenever Savage was under attack, his manager Miss Elizabeth would find Hogan and bring him to the rescue.

The Mega Powers had much success and were on their way to winning the WWE Tag Team Championship. However, Savage began to suspect Hogan was going to steal Miss Elizabeth's affections and managerial services away from him. Savage attacked Hogan, accidentally injuring Miss Elizabeth in the process. The Mega Powers split and ended their rivalry at *WrestleMania V*, when Hogan won the WWE Championship.

Earthquake

Weighing nearly 500lbs (226kg), Earthquake was a dangerous WWE rookie who crushed his opponents by jumping and sitting on their chests. He had one objective: end Hogan's career. On the May 26, 1990 episode of *WWE Superstars*, Earthquake attacked Hogan from behind and sat on Hogan's chest, breaking several of his ribs. It seemed that Earthquake had succeeded in his goal. However, Hogan recovered and made his return on the July 14 episode of *WWE Superstars*. He challenged Earthquake to a match at *SummerSlam* a month later. During the match Hogan got his revenge by slamming Earthquake through a table and getting the win.

Ultimate Warrior

WWE Champion Hulk Hogan and Intercontinental Champion Ultimate Warrior were signed for a match at *WrestleMania VI,* with the winner receiving both Titles. The two Superstars had been friends since Warrior joined WWE two years earlier. However, as their match drew closer, their friendship was put on hold as their competitive natures took over. In the match itself, both fought hard, but in the end, it was Warrior who came out on top. Hogan handed Warrior the Title, raising his hand in a show of respect.

JAKE "THE SNAKE" ROBERTS

VS.

RICKY "THE DRAGON" STEAMBOAT

Jake "The Snake" Roberts and Ricky "The Dragon" Steamboat were two of WWE's biggest stars when their paths crossed in 1986. They both reflected their nicknames and mascots: Roberts was sneaky, slithering, and would strike when least expected; Steamboat was majestic, dangerous, and wowed the WWE Universe with his high-flying in-ring moves. Their personalities were destined for conflict, bringing about one of the greatest rivalries of the year.

"Don't you understand? I don't watch the game. I don't play the game ... I rule the game."

WWE on MSG Network, May 17, 1986

1. A slippery end
Saturday Night's Main Event,
May 3, 1986: Ricky "The Dragon" Steamboat was set to face Jake "The Snake" Roberts, but before the match officially began, Roberts struck. He spiked Steamboat with a devastating DDT move on the ringside floor. Roberts then brought out his massive python Damien, letting the huge snake wrap around Steamboat's prone body.

2. Seeking revenge
WWE **on** ***MSG Network*, May 19, 1986:**
Just two weeks after Roberts' first ringside attack on Steamboat, the pair met again at the legendary Madison Square Garden arena. The action spilled out of the ring, and Roberts tried yet another DDT maneuver on the hard floor. Steamboat escaped Roberts this time, and the entire WWE locker came out to pull the rivals apart. The referee ultimately disqualified both Roberts and Steamboat for their behavior.

3. In-ring chaos

Boston, August 9, 1986: In yet another vicious battle, the referee was accidentally struck down by the Superstars. Roberts pinned Steamboat, but the referee couldn't complete the count. Steamboat reversed the move and pinned Roberts as the referee came to. Frustrated at the loss, Roberts hit his rival with yet another DDT move.

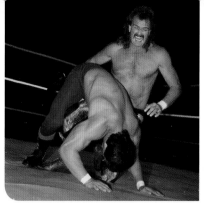

4. The pit

WWE Big Event, August 28, 1986: Roberts challenged Steamboat to compete against him in a Snake Pit Match—a match where there are no rules. Roberts tried attacking Steamboat before the match again, but Steamboat was ready for it this time. The two hit each other with everything they had. In a repeat of their earlier encounter, Roberts pinned Steamboat only for Steamboat to reverse the pin and get the win.

> **"I put my dragon 'Creature Feature' face to face with Jake Roberts, and that man took a step backward faster than anyone I've seen in my life."**
>
> *WWE on MSG Network*
> August 30, 1986

5. Enter the dragon

Saturday Night's Main Event, October 4, 1986: Returning to the show where it all started, Roberts and Steamboat battled in another no-rules Snake Pit Match. This time, Steamboat brought his pet Komodo dragon to the ring with him. Roberts got Steamboat outside the ring and was about to DDT him when Steamboat slipped away. Steamboat grabbed his mascot and chased Roberts and his python off, winning the match and ending this reptilian rivalry.

RIVAL FACTS

- Ricky Steamboat and Jake Roberts were both inducted into the WWE Hall of Fame, with Steamboat entering in 2009 and Roberts in 2014.

- Ricky Steamboat won the Intercontinental Championship once, but Jake Roberts never won a WWE title.

HARLEY RACE

VS.

JUNKYARD DOG

Harley Race won the World Heavyweight Championship in National Wrestling Alliance in 1973 before entering WWE. He considered himself as tough as nails, had no remorse for those he beat, and no regrets for the violent tactics that earned him his victories. Junkyard Dog (JYD) was a man of the people who loved to dance in the ring with fans after matches. He did his best to protect and defend those threatened by Superstars such as Harley Race.

> "Either the Junkyard Dog will bow before the king, or they will carry him out from the ring."
>
> *WWE on MSG Network,* January 19, 1987

1. King Harley Race

***King of the Ring**, July 14, 1986:* Harley Race defeated three other Superstars to become the King of the Ring in WWE. With great arrogance, Race demanded his vanquished opponents bow before him at the end of their matches. He believed, as King of WWE, he was entitled to such adulation and worship. JYD disagreed, promising he would never bow to Race.

2. The Dog bites

Saturday Night's Main Event, **January 3, 1987:** JYD got his first chance to show King Harley Race he wouldn't bow to him at *Saturday Night's Main Event*. As Race lay outside the ring recovering from a JYD attack, JYD took Race's robe and crown and wore them mockingly. Race and his manager Bobby "The Brain" Heenan attacked JYD, getting Race disqualified. Heenan and Race tried to force JYD to bow, but he fought back defiantly.

"This country ain't had no king. This country ain't had no queen. Harley Race, who you think you're dealing with?"

Saturday Night's Main Event,
January 3, 1987

3. Sore loser

WWE on MSG Network, **January 19, 1987:**
JYD wanted a rematch against Race, and he got it. The animosity between the two was clear as the Superstars fought viciously outside the ring. JYD heard the referee counting and slid back into the ring before he was counted out; however, King Race didn't make it back in time and lost by countout. Angered by this, Race then challenged JYD to a Loser Must Bow Match at the upcoming *WrestleMania III*.

4. Six-Man Tag Elimination Match

WWE on MSG Network, **February 23, 1987:** Junkyard Dog joined with "Rowdy" Roddy Piper and Ricky "The Dragon" Steamboat to face their respective upcoming *WrestleMania III* opponents: King Harley Race, Adrian Adonis, and "Macho Man" Randy Savage. Although Junkyard Dog was eliminated early in the match, his team won the contest when Roddy Piper pinned Randy Savage.

5. Loser MustBow Match

WrestleMania III, **March 29, 1987:**
King Harley Race made his way to the ring, accompanied by his manager Bobby Heenan and the "Queen" of WWE: The Fabulous Moolah. Moolah and Heenan cheated to help Race pin JYD. At the end of the match, Moolah placed Race's crown on his head, but JYD refused to bow before Race. Instead, JYD hit Race with a chair and put on the crown and robe himself!

JAKE "THE SNAKE" ROBERTS

VS.

"RAVISHING" RICK RUDE

There weren't many Superstars who dared cross tough guy Jake "The Snake" Roberts, but "Ravishing" Rick Rude found a reason to. Rude considered himself a ladies' man. He insulted male Superstars and fans before every match, and believed himself irresistible to all women. At least he did until he met Roberts' wife Cheryl. When she publicly rejected him, Rude swore revenge on Jake "The Snake" as a way of avenging this blow to his reputation.

RIVAL FACTS

● Rude was a two-time Intercontinental Champion in WWE, while Roberts never won any championships.

● Rude and Roberts competed against each other in the first round of *WrestleMania IV*'s WWE Championship tournament. However, the match resulted in a time-limit draw, so neither man advanced in the tournament.

● Roberts was inducted into the WWE Hall of Fame in 2014; Rude received that honor in 2017.

> "Rick Rude, we're not talking about fighting for a pile of money... We're talking about what makes me happy."
>
> *Superstars*, October 16, 1988

1. Dangerous flirting

Superstars, **April 16, 1988:** After every one of his matches, Rude would approach a female member of the WWE Universe who inevitably would swoon and kiss him. But on this night, Rude made the wrong choice. The woman sitting on the front row flatly rejected his advances, revealing she was married to Jake "The Snake" Roberts. Rude did not take the rejection gracefully, so Roberts raced to ringside to defend his wife, Cheryl.

2. Not man enough

Superstars, June 11, 1988:
Roberts and his wife Cheryl sat down for an interview to discuss Rude's flirtations. Both of them dismissed Rude's claims to be a "real man," saying that Rick wasn't man enough to be with Cheryl, nor man enough to defeat Roberts in the ring. Cheryl even said she pitied Rude for what Roberts was going to do to him.

> "Jake Roberts is nothing but a sleazy, lowdown, worthless piece of garbage."
>
> Superstars, April 16, 1988

3. Love and war

Wrestling Challenge, July 10, 1988:
Rude and his manager Bobby "The Brain" Heenan appeared on the Brother Love talk show segment, where Rude declared he was going to free Cheryl from Roberts, allegedly so she could fulfill her fantasies of being with him. Rude claimed that he knew Cheryl was really in love with him, not Roberts, and soon she would be his.

4. Face off

Wrestling Challenge, August 23, 1988:
To further demonstrate his affection for Cheryl and play mind games with Roberts, Rude started wearing tights that featured Cheryl's face printed on them. The tights enraged Roberts; he would charge into the ring and tear the tights off Rude every time he wore them.

5. A true finisher

WWE on MSG Network, October 24, 1988: The rivalry came to a head at Madison Square Garden. Rude and Roberts fought in a match where the first Superstar to execute his finishing maneuver would be declared the winner. Rude tried to execute his Rude Awakening move by pulling Roberts back-to-back, but was unable to. Roberts then successfully hit Rude with his winning DDT move. Following the match, Cheryl slapped Rude repeatedly and Jake's pet snake slithered all over Rude's fallen body.

DUSTY RHODES

VS.

"MILLION DOLLAR MAN" TED DIBIASE

Dusty Rhodes proudly referred to himself as "The American Dream." The son of a plumber, Rhodes worked his way up from humble origins to become a successful Superstar. He represented the common man, working hard for all he achieved. In contrast, "Million Dollar Man" Ted DiBiase reveled in his wealth and mocked Rhodes' upbringing. Rhodes was determined to show DiBiase that money can't buy worth or happiness. He would show everyone that hard work and confidence mattered more.

DID YOU KNOW?

DiBiase's and Rhodes' sons, Ted DiBiase and Cody Rhodes. formed the tag team Legacy in 2008.

"A bond between a father and a son ... cannot be bought, baby."

Superstars, December 22, 1990

RIVAL FACTS

● Rhodes was inducted into the WWE Hall of Fame in 2007; DiBiase was inducted in 2010.

● In appreciation of his contributions to WWE and sports entertainment, a bronze statue of Rhodes was unveiled during 2016's *WrestleMania* 32 weekend.

1. Priceless debut

Boston Garden, June 3, 1989:
For decades, Dusty Rhodes had competed in WWE's rival organization WCW, becoming a World Heavyweight Champion there. When he joined WWE, his first match was against "Million Dollar Man" Ted DiBiase. DiBiase, who thought he could buy every win, tried offering Rhodes hundreds of dollars to forfeit the match. Dusty offered the money to members of the WWE Universe and then beat DiBiase, and his manager Virgil, in the match.

2. Public humiliation

SummerSlam, August 27, 1990:
DiBiase had been humiliated by Rhodes after their first match and sought revenge. Just as Rhodes was due to start a match against Randy Savage, DiBiase appeared ringside along with Rhodes' manager Sweet Sapphire. DiBiase announced that he had purchased Sapphire's services for himself. Rhodes was so distracted he lost his match. Later Rhodes chased after his rival and former manager as they left in DiBiase's limousine.

3. Elimination attempt

Survivor Series, November 22, 1990:
The stakes were raised as Rhodes and DiBiase each put together teams to compete in a *Survivor Series* Elimination Match. The Million Dollar Team (DiBiase, Honkey Tonk Man, Greg Valentine, and Undertaker) defeated the Dream Team (Rhodes, Bret Hart, Jim "The Anvil" Neidhart, and Koko B. Ware) after DiBiase eliminated Bret Hart. This victory did not satisy DiBiase, however, who still wanted payback for his original humiliation.

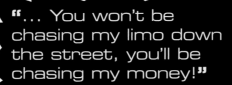

> "... You won't be chasing my limo down the street, you'll be chasing my money!"
>
> *Wrestling Challenge,* September 30, 1990

4. Brother Love Show

Superstars, December 22, 1990:
DiBiase's next attempt to belittle Rhodes involved Rhodes' son, Dustin. Not for the first time, DiBiase made financial offers to Dustin, which were refused. In return, father and son appeared on the Brother Love talk show segment and challenged DiBiase and his manager Virgil to a tag team match at the upcoming *Royal Rumble* pay-per-view.

5. Final match

Royal Rumble, January 19, 1991: DiBiase and Virgil accepted The Rhodes Family's challenge, and competed in a tag team match. Dusty and Dustin attacked Virgil together, which angered DiBiase. DiBiase berated Virgil and attacked both the Rhodes men himself. In the end, DiBiase surprised Dusty with a roll-up pin, winning the match. Rhodes retired from full-time in-ring competition following the match.

BOY NOT FOR SALE

Ted DiBiase made several attempts to "buy" Dusty Rhodes' son Dustin, including:

Saturday Night's Main Event (October 13, 1990) As Dustin sat ringside watching his father, DiBiase and Virgil offered him cash to sit in his seat. Rhodes ripped up the money and threw it back. Enraged, DiBiase attacked Dustin.

Superstars (November 3, 1990) DiBiase challenged Dustin to a "Ten Minute Challenge." If Dustin couldn't last 10 minutes in the ring with DiBiase, he'd join DiBiase's team. Dusty coached Dustin throughout the match, helping his son beat the time limit and reject another DiBiase offer.

Superstars (December 8, 1990) Dustin was being interviewed on the Brother Love Show when DiBiase and Virgil interrupted the segment. DiBiase offered Rhodes hundreds of dollars to become his newest employee. Dustin again refused, swatting the money out of DiBiase's hands. DiBiase and Virgil pummeled Dustin in response.

DEMOLITION VS. LEGION OF DOOM

These two legendary tag teams seemed to be from some postapocalyptic hellscape. Both Demolition (Ax, Smash, and Crush) and the Legion of Doom (Road Warrior Hawk and Road Warrior Animal) were ruthless with opponents, and each team accused the other of being imposters. The Legion had competed around the world before Demolition was formed, but Demolition were multi-time WWE Tag Team Champions before the Legion arrived on the scene.

> **"Legion of Doom ... Well, we're going to kick that paint right off your face."**
> —Ax, *Wrestling Challenge*, July 15, 1990

1. It's Doomsday

Wrestling Challenge, **July 15, 1990:**
The Legion of Doom made their WWE debut, decimating a pair of rookies, Alan Reynolds and Bob Bradley, and showing the WWE Universe what they were capable of. During the match, Demolition spoke to the announcers in a split screen, calling the Legion of Doom "Demolition Imposters," and warning them to stay away. The Legion of Doom would do anything but.

DID YOU KNOW?
Demolition are the second longest reigning Tag Team Champions in WWE history, behind The New Day.

2. Tag team cheats

SummerSlam, **August 27, 1990:**
Demolition were defending their Championship against the Hart Foundation. Smash and Crush were competing in the match. Partway through, the third member, Ax, sneakily switched places with Smash. The Legion of Doom raced to ringside, attacking Demolition, exposing their cheating, and costing them the Tag Team Championship.

3. Brother hater

Superstars, September 15, 1990: WWE talk show host Brother Love brought the Legion of Doom out as his guests to criticize them for interfering in Demolition's tag team match. Hawk and Animal replied that they weren't afraid of Demolition, even if it was three-on-two.

> **"Demolition, you are going to feel the wrath of the supreme force— the Legion of Doom!"**
>
> —Road Warrior Animal, *Superstars,* August 25, 1990

4. Crush, crushed!

***WWE on MSG Network,* January 21, 1991:** Demolition attacked the Legion of Doom before Hawk and Animal could take their spiked shoulder pads off for the match. From there, Demolition looked for shortcuts to a win, including having their manager Mr. Fuji hit Hawk with his walking cane. Legion of Doom overcame the cheating and pinned Demolition's Crush for three.

SIX-MAN TAG TEAM MATCH

In their battle against the three-man team of Demolition's Ax, Smash, and Crush, the Legion of Doom often added face-painted WWE Champion Ultimate Warrior and fought in Six-Man Tag Team Matches against Demolition.

Saturday Night's Main Event (September 18, 1990) Road Warrior Hawk, Road Warrior Animal, and Ultimate Warrior were victorious over Demolition.

WWE on MSG Network (September 21, 1990) The Legion of Doom and Ultimate Warrior destroyed Demolition.

Superstars (October 9, 1990) Ultimate Warrior and LOD defeated Demolition again.

Survivor Series (November 22, 1990) Ultimate Warrior, Texas Tornado, and Legion of Doom beat Mr. Perfect and Demolition in a traditional *Survivor Series* Elimination Match.

5. Demolition derby

***Wrestling Challenge,* February 10, 1991:** After months of competing against each other, it was the final match between the Legion of Doom and Demolition. Hawk and Animal dominated the match. Mr. Fuji prevented Hawk from flying from the top to hit his Doomsday Device move, but the Legion of Doom still defeated Demolition. Demolition slunk away from the ring while the Legion of Doom celebrated, proving once and for all who was the dominant team.

"RAVISHING" RICK RUDE

VS.

ULTIMATE WARRIOR

"Ravishing" Rick Rude and Ultimate Warrior were both known for their incredible physiques. In fact, each man boasted that he had the very best body in all of WWE. These boastful statements brought them into direct conflict with each other. While it was never definitively determined who had the greatest body, one of the two clearly proved his in-ring dominance.

252lbs (114.30kg)

DID YOU KNOW?

Rick Rude gave Ultimate Warrior his very first loss in WWE when he defeated him at *WrestleMania V.*

"It's like this, Warrior ... I'm gonna step over your carcass and walk out the cage door."

Superstars, July 22, 1990

1. Striking a pose

***Royal Rumble**, January 15, 1989:* Intercontinental Champion Ultimate Warrior and "Ravishing" Rick Rude were invited to show off their muscular bodies in a "Posedown." The winner would be decided by who got the most audience cheers in each of four categories: Biceps, Abs, Most Muscular, and Medley of Poses. Warrior won each category, and an enraged Rude attacked him with a workout bar.

2. A Rude intervention

***WrestleMania V**, April 2, 1989:* To get revenge on Rude for the workout bar attack, Warrior put his Intercontinental Championship on the line against him at *WrestleMania V*. Rude tried attacking Warrior before the match, but injured his knee on Warrior's Title. The match ended when Rude's manager Bobby "The Brain" Heenan tripped Warrior, allowing Rude to get the pin and win the Intercontinental Championship.

3. Warrior strikes back

SummerSlam, **August 28, 1989:** Warrior was entitled to a rematch for the Intercontinental Championship. Warrior used a variety of attacks against Rude and his manager Bobby Heenan, but it wasn't until "Rowdy" Roddy Piper came to ringside to distract Rude and Heenan that Warrior was able to defeat Rude and win back the Intercontinental Championship.

"You, 'Ravishing' Rick Rude, will surrender when I beat you one, two, three!"

SummerSlam, August 28, 1989

280lbs (127kg)

4. A meddling manager

Saturday Night's Main Event, **July 28, 1990:** Warrior had won the WWE Championship at *WrestleMania VI*. His old rival Rude returned seeking the Title. Rude got his first chance at *Saturday Night's Main Event*. As Warrior was about to get a pin victory, Rude's manager Bobby Heenan attacked him, interrupting the pin and getting Rude disqualified.

WEAKENING THE WARRIOR

Leading up to their match at 1989's *SummerSlam*, "Ravishing" Rick Rude and his manager Bobby "The Brain" Heenan had other Superstars he managed attack the Ultimate Warrior in order to "soften him up" for Rude.

Prime Time Wrestling (August 13, 1989) Haku faced Ultimate Warrior in an official match, and was defeated. Rick Rude and André the Giant also came to ringside to help with the attack, but Warrior simply threw Rude onto André.

Superstars (August 26, 1989) André the Giant hit Ultimate Warrior from behind and, while Warrior was distracted by Bobby Heenan, used his vast strength to knock him out with a nerve pinch.

5. Out the cage door

SummerSlam, **August 27, 1990:** To prevent further interference from Rude's manager Bobby "The Brain" Heenan, Warrior defended his WWE Championship against Rude in a steel cage. As the Warrior was about to escape the cage, Heenan slammed the door on him. Warrior dropped Heenan with a hit and slammed Rude before escaping the cage to win the match and keep his Championship.

DUSTY RHODES VS. "MACHO KING" RANDY SAVAGE

After defeating the reigning King of the Ring Jim Duggan, Randy Savage changed his nickname from "Macho Man" to "Macho King." He strutted around wearing a crown and carrying a scepter, while arrogantly belittling the "common folk." There was no one more "common" than Dusty Rhodes. Going by the moniker "The American Dream," Rhodes, alongside his manager Sweet Sapphire, targeted Savage and his manager Sensational Queen Sherri, ready to prove that commoners always beat royalty.

RIVAL FACTS

● Dusty Rhodes never won any titles in WWE, while Randy Savage was a former World and Intercontinental Champion.

● Dusty Rhodes and Randy Savage are both WWE Hall of Famers. Rhodes was inducted in 2007 and Savage in 2015.

1. No love lost
Royal Rumble,
January 21, 1990: WWE talk show host Brother Love invited Sensational Queen Sherri and Sweet Sapphire onto his show, and he and Sherri proceeded to make fun of Sapphire. Sapphire finally snapped and attacked Sherri. Dusty Rhodes and Randy Savage then raced to the ring to protect their respective managers and brawled with each other, until WWE officials pulled them apart.

2. Victory dance
Ultimate Challenge Special,
March 25, 1990: Rhodes and Sapphire agreed to face Savage and Sherri in the first ever Mixed Tag Team Match at *WrestleMania VI*. But a week before, Rhodes and Savage battled one-on-one. Rhodes hit Savage with his Bionic Elbow and was winning when Sherri jumped on him. Savage was disqualified and he and Sherri were sent to the dressing room, while Sapphire and Rhodes celebrated.

3. Tag team showdown

WrestleMania VI, **April 1, 1990:** As they entered the ring for their Mixed Tag Team Match against Savage and Sherri, Rhodes and Sapphire brought with them a secret weapon they called the "Crown Jewels" to distract Savage—none other than Elizabeth, Savage's former manager. Elizabeth was an effective weapon against Savage because, although they'd split professionally and romantically a year earlier, deep down Savage still loved her. Savage tried hitting Rhodes with his scepter, but with Elizabeth's help, Rhodes and Sapphire defeated Savage and Sherri.

> "... Dusty Rhodes can only fantasize about what it's like to be the 'Macho King' Randy Savage!"
>
> *Wrestling Challenge*, June 24, 1990

4. Savage attack

Superstars, **April 14, 1990:** Dusty Rhodes and Sapphire had entered the ring dancing to their entrance music when, out of nowhere, Savage and Sherri attacked them from behind. Sherri beat on Sapphire and Savage climbed to the top rope three times, each time diving off and hitting Rhodes with his signature Elbow Drop move.

BATTLE OF THE MANAGERS

Sherri and Sapphire had a series of one-on-one matches where they battled over personal pride.

Richmond, Virginia (April 21, 1990) Sherri, accompanied to the ring by Savage, pinned Sapphire for a three count to get the first win.

Fort Myers, Florida (June 1, 1990) Sapphire got her first victory over Sherri albeit by disqualification when Savage attacked the referee.

Kitchener, Ontario, Canada (June 17, 1990) Two weeks after Sapphire's first victory, Sherri got her revenge by again pinning her to the mat.

5. Counted out

SummerSlam, **August 27, 1990:** At *SummerSlam*, Rhodes was pitted against Savage, and Sapphire against Sherri, in one-on-one matches. Sapphire didn't show up for her match, giving Sherri a forfeit win. Worried, Rhodes went looking for Sapphire backstage. Just as his match was about to begin, "Million Dollar Man" Ted DiBiase announced that Sapphire was now working for him. Savage used this distraction to attack Rhodes and pin him for the three count.

JAKE "THE SNAKE" ROBERTS
VS.
UNDERTAKER

Jake "The Snake" Roberts and Undertaker both enjoyed using nasty methods to win matches and torment their rivals. Although their matching appetites for evil initially drew them into a grim friendship, they later split in spectacular style, leading to a confrontation that truly plumbed new depths of darkness.

THE MAKEUP

1. Joining forces

After being locked in a coffin by Undertaker, Ultimate Warrior asked Jake "The Snake" Roberts to teach him how to exist on the darkside so he would be ready for Undertaker next time. On August 17, 1991, Roberts put the Warrior through a series of trials that made him confront his fears. In the final trial, Roberts tricked Warrior into being bitten by a deadly cobra before revealing that he'd been working with Undertaker the entire time.

> "Undertaker, when the time comes, I will put the final nail in your own coffin. Trust me."
>
> *WrestleMania VIII*, April 5, 1992

2. The wedding reception

SummerSlam, August 26, 1991: Undertaker and Roberts again joined forces to bring darkness to WWE when they attacked the wedding reception of Randy "Macho Man" Savage and his bride, Elizabeth. Roberts and Undertaker had hidden a cobra in one of their gifts, and physically assaulted Savage with Undertaker's urn. They were only turned back when Sid Justice fought them out of the reception.

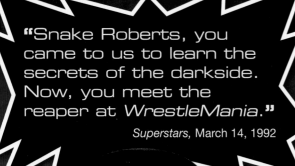

> "Snake Roberts, you came to us to learn the secrets of the darkside. Now, you meet the reaper at *WrestleMania*."
>
> *Superstars*, March 14, 1992

THE BREAKUP

3. Change of heart

After losing to Randy "Macho Man" Savage, a livid Roberts waited backstage, ready to hit Savage and his wife Elizabeth with a chair. As Elizabeth entered the backstage area, Roberts tried to swing the chair, but something stopped him. Undertaker had grabbed the chair, giving Savage a chance to retaliate. Undertaker sneered as he stood over the fallen body of his former ally.

DID YOU KNOW?

Undertaker's victory over Roberts at *WrestleMania VIII* was the second win in his 21-year undefeated *WrestleMania* streak.

4. Battle at the funeral parlor

***Superstars*, February 29, 1992:** Roberts confronted Undertaker on Paul Bearer's talk show, asking why Undertaker had stopped his attack on Elizabeth and demaded to know whose side he was on. "Not yours!" was Undertaker's stark reply. Enraged, Roberts locked Undertaker's hand in a casket and beat him with a chair. Much to Roberts' fury, Undertaker wouldn't stay down.

5. Burying The Snake

***WrestleMania VIII*, April 5, 1992:** Roberts entered his match against Undertaker at *WrestleMania VIII* with all the confidence in the world. It counted for nothing, because it was Undertaker who proved dominant. Although Roberts was able to land his finishing move (the DDT) on Undertaker twice, Undertaker just wouldn't be stopped. He hit Roberts with the Tombstone and pinned him for the three count.

RIVAL FACTS

● Undertaker has won 15 championships in WWE, including seven WWE World Heavyweight Championships. Roberts never won a single title.

● After returning to WWE in 1996, Roberts occasionally joined Undertaker in tag team matches, facing teams such as Shawn Michaels and Diesel as well as Mankind and Goldust.

● Roberts was inducted into the WWE Hall of Fame in 2014. Undertaker is sure to receive the same honor in due time.

"MACHO KING" RANDY SAVAGE

VS.

ULTIMATE WARRIOR

Two of the most colorful Superstars—in personality and in dress—to ever compete in WWE, "Macho King" Randy Savage and Ultimate Warrior were bitter foes, whose disdain for each other drove them both to the very edge of madness. Each confrontation in and out of the ring only increased the intensity of their mutual loathing. They battled in high-energy, fast-paced matches that required both of them to give their best.

THE BREAKUP

"I will beat you, Ultimate Warrior, with a one, two, three count. I guarantee it. Dig it!"

Superstars, August 29, 1992

1. The challenges
Ultimate Warrior won the WWE Championship at *WrestleMania VI* in April 1990. Right away, "Macho King" Randy Savage's manager, Sensational Queen Sherri, began to confront the Warrior repeatedly on Savage's behalf, demanding a Championship Match. The Warrior rejected all her requests immediately, earning him Savage's growing ire.

2. Crowned!
Royal Rumble, January 19, 1991: After Warrior again rejected Savage's challenge for a WWE Championship Match, "The Macho King" and Sensational Queen Sherri attacked him during his Championship Match against Sgt. Slaughter. Savage smashed his golden scepter down on Warrior, causing Warrior to lose the match and the Championship. The move left the crowd almost as stunned as Warrior.

3. Career-ending match

WrestleMania VII, March 24, 1991:
The anger between Warrior and Savage escalated quickly and explosively. A drastic resolution was clearly needed. It was decided that they would face each other at *WrestleMania*—the loser being forced to retire from WWE. With everything on the line, the two combatants fought with all they had for their careers, but it was the Warrior who came out on top, forcing Savage into retirement.

4. Final battle

SummerSlam, August 29, 1992:
Emerging from retirement, Randy Savage beat WWE Champion Ric Flair for the Title at *WrestleMania VIII*. His first Title defense was against his old rival—Ultimate Warrior. Their enmity reignited, Warrior and Savage pummeled each other mercilessly for several minutes until Ric Flair and his associate Mr. Perfect interfered. The result was a countout win, but not a Title win, for the Warrior.

> **"The Ultimate Warrior fears no Macho Man!"**
> *Superstars*, September 8, 1990

ULTIMATE MANIACS

The Ultimate Maniacs were only together for a short time, but were a memorable and successful tag team in WWE.

SummerSlam Spectacular (August 23, 1992) Warrior and Savage's first team-up was against the Nasty Boys, The Ultimate Maniacs losing by count out after being attacked by Ric Flair and Mr. Perfect.

Live Event (October 12, 1992) The Ultimate Maniacs defeated Tag Team Champions Money Inc. by countout in a nontitle match.

Saturday Night's Main Event (November 14, 1992) The Ultimate Maniacs had a shot at the Tag Team Championship, but Champions Money Inc. walked out of the match, being counted out but not losing the Titles.

THE MAKEUP

5. Time to team up

Following 1992's *SummerSlam*, Warrior and Randy Savage, who was once again calling himself Macho Man, ended their rivalry in a surprising way. They formed a tag team, first to seek revenge on Ric Flair and Mr. Perfect, then to rise to the top of the WWE Tag Team Division. As The Ultimate Maniacs, they won several matches, proving that the worst of rivals could become the best of teammates.

HART FOUNDATION

VS.

NASTY BOYS

Brothers-in-law Bret "Hit Man" Hart and Jim "The Anvil" Neidhart joined up with legendary manager Jimmy Hart (no relation) to form the Hart Foundation. Jimmy led the Hart Foundation to great success, but when they lost the Tag Team Championship, Jimmy Hart dumped the Hart Foundation in favor of other tag teams. Among Hart's new signees were the Nasty Boys—Brian Knobs and Jerry Sags—who set out to prove that they were better than the Harts.

1. Recapturing the gold

SummerSlam, August 27, 1990:
The Hart Foundation defeated Demolition in a Two Out of Three Falls Match to win their second Tag Team Championship, this time without their former manager Jimmy Hart. They would go on to defend the Title against the very best tag teams in WWE, including The Rockers, Power and Glory, and Rhythm & Blues.

2. Nasty Boys arrive

Superstars, December 29, 1990:
Jimmy Hart looked all over the world to find a new tag team to challenge the Hart Foundation. He founded the Nasty Boys, calling them the hottest, nastiest tag team he'd ever managed. The Nasty Boys defeated rookies Jimmy Evans and Sonny Blaze in their debut match, and warned the WWE Universe and Superstars that things were about to get nasty!

"Your time has come, Hart Foundation, and it's nasty!"
—Jerry Sags, *WrestleMania VII*, March 24, 1991

3. Number one contenders

Superstars, **February 16, 1991:**
The Nasty Boys competed in a Ta
Team Battle Royal, with the winne
receiving a Tag Team Championsh
Match against the Hart Foundatio
at *WrestleMania VII*. The Nasty Bc
won the Battle Royal Match and
became number one contenders
when rival tag teams Power and
Glory and the Legion of Doom
eliminated each other.

4. Nasty champs

WrestleMania VII, **March 24, 1991:**
The Nasty Boys were hyped and
ready for their match against the Hart
Foundation. But the Hart Foundation
refused to go down without a fight.
Different from most of the Hart
Foundation's matches, which were
characterized by in-ring technical
ability, this was a battle. Both teams
exchanged blows. The Nasty Boys
won the match and the Tag Team
Championship when Jerry Sags used
manager Jimmy Hart's motorcycle
helmet to knock down Jim Neidhart.

5. One chance

WWE on MSG Network, **July 1, 1991:**
The Hart Foundation were granted one rematcl
against the Nasty Boys to try to win back the
WWE Tag Team Championship. Bret hit the
Nasty Boys with the same motorcycle helmet
Sags had used at *WrestleMania*. Only this time
the referee saw the helmet attack and the
match ended in a disqualification win for
the Champion Nasty Boys.

JAKE "THE SNAKE" ROBERTS

VS.

RANDY "MACHO MAN" SAVAGE

Jake "The Snake" Roberts was a master manipulator who liked to use mind games—and his pet snakes—to frighten opponents. He set his sights on Randy "Macho Man" Savage and belittled him, believing that he wouldn't fight back. After all, Savage had retired from in-ring competition. However, Savage had other ideas.

"Now you look into my eyes, Randy Savage, and you'll see something so cold, so devilish, and so deliberate—yes, he takes care of what he has to."

This Tuesday in Texas, December 3, 1991

1. Wedding crasher

***SummerSlam*, August 26, 1991:** Following their in-ring wedding at *SummerSlam*, Randy "Macho Man" Savage and Miss Elizabeth celebrated their nuptials with a grand reception. As the happy couple opened their gifts, they were horrified when a cobra leaped out of a box and tried to bite Elizabeth. Seconds later, Jake "The Snake" Roberts burst into the reception. He chased Savage with the cobra, traumatizing Elizabeth.

2. Cobra bite

***Superstars*, November 23, 1991:** Following a match against a rookie, Roberts grabbed a microphone and berated Savage. Savage, who, as one of the show's regular announcers, was sitting at the commentators' table, charged the ring. Roberts tackled Savage, tangling him in the ring ropes. He then pulled out a giant king cobra, which fastened onto Savage's arm.

3. Randy's return

Superstars, **November 30, 1991:** Since he'd been forced to retire after losing to Ultimate Warrior at *WrestleMania VII*, Savage wasn't allowed to get revenge on Roberts for his repeated assaults. For several months, Savage lobbied WWE officials to reinstate him. The king cobra attack finally convinced WWE President Jack Tunney to reinstate Savage, effective immediately.

RIVAL FACTS

● Savage won WWE and Intercontinental Championships, something that Roberts admitted he was jealous of, since he never won any championships during his time in WWE.

● Roberts and Savage were inducted into the WWE Hall of Fame one year apart—Roberts in 2014, Savage in 2015.

> **"Snake man ... It's time for you to find out how insane I am! Yeah!"**
>
> *Saturday Night's Main Event,*
> February 8, 1991

4. Sore loser

This Tuesday in Texas, **December 3, 1991:** Three days after being reinstated, Savage was granted a match against Roberts. Savage didn't waste any time, giving Roberts a brutal pounding and using his flying elbow finisher to get the victory. After the match, however, Roberts attacked Savage, making his wife Elizabeth beg for mercy, before WWE officials escorted Roberts from the ring.

5. Savaging the Snake

Saturday Night's Main Event, **February 8, 1992:** Savage and Roberts had a final confrontation which was just as brutal as previous encounters. After they exchanged painful blows, Savage hit Roberts with his flying elbow for a pinfall victory. Afterward, Savage continued to pummel Roberts, until officials pulled him away and Roberts escaped to the back of the auditorium.

MR. PERFECT
VS.
"NATURE BOY" RIC FLAIR

There's a reason "Nature Boy" Ric Flair's motto was "kiss-stealing, wheelin' 'n' dealin', limousine riding, jet flying, son of a gun." Flair clearly relished the finer things. When he joined WWE, Flair found a kindred spirit in Mr. Perfect, who excelled at everything he did, including partying. Flair and Perfect seemed almost as close as brothers. But their friendship was not to last.

DID YOU KNOW?

Both Ric Flair and Mr. Perfect were managed by legendary manager Bobby "The Brain" Heenan.

1. The consultant

Superstars, **November 24, 1991:** Since joining WWE earlier in 1991, Flair had been managed by Bobby Heenan. Heading into *Survivor Series*, in which Flair led a stable who were due to battle "Rowdy" Roddy Piper's team, Flair announced Heenan would no longer be his manager. Instead, Mr. Perfect would serve as an Executive Consultant, helping Flair to cheat to win matches—and make everything just "Perfect."

2. Tension mounts

Prime Time Wrestling, **October 12, 1992:** When Ric Flair lost the WWE Championship to Bret "Hit Man" Hart, tension began to rise between Flair and Perfect. Flair started blaming Perfect for his defeats and reminding Perfect that he worked for him. Flair declared that Perfect "walked in his shadow." Mr. Perfect resented this jibe, but tried to keep his feelings in check for the good of the team.

RIVAL FACTS

- Both Ric Flair and Mr. Perfect grew up in Minneapolis, Minnesota.

- Mr. Perfect is a two-time Intercontinental Champion; Ric Flair won the Intercontinental Championship once.

- Flair is a 16-time World Champion, but Mr. Perfect never won a World Title.

- Mr. Perfect was inducted into the WWE Hall of Fame in 2007. Flair followed a year later.

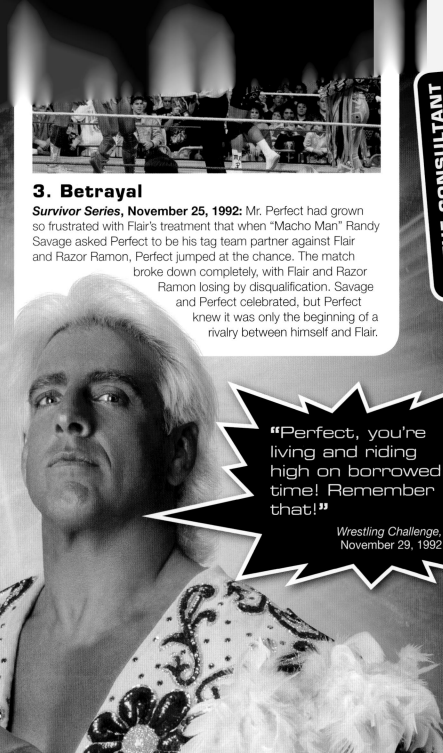

3. Betrayal

Survivor Series, **November 25, 1992:** Mr. Perfect had grown so frustrated with Flair's treatment that when "Macho Man" Randy Savage asked Perfect to be his tag team partner against Flair and Razor Ramon, Perfect jumped at the chance. The match broke down completely, with Flair and Razor Ramon losing by disqualification. Savage and Perfect celebrated, but Perfect knew it was only the beginning of a rivalry between himself and Flair.

> **"Perfect, you're living and riding high on borrowed time! Remember that!"**
>
> *Wrestling Challenge,*
> November 29, 1992

4. The Perfect elimination

Royal Rumble, **January 24, 1993:** Ric Flair and Mr. Perfect had both entered the Royal Rumble Match, hoping for a shot at the WWE Championship at *WrestleMania*. During the 30-man contest, Perfect clotheslined Flair, sending him over the top rope and to the arena floor, eliminating him from the match.

5. So long Nature Boy

RAW, **January 25, 1993:** The night after the *Royal Rumble*, Ric Flair made a declaration: WWE wasn't big enough for both him and Mr. Perfect. The two competed in a Loser Leaves Town Match that night, where the loser would be forced to leave WWE. Both Superstars fought with all their heart to keep their career intact. In the end, Mr. Perfect pinned Ric Flair, sending the "Nature Boy" packing.

RAZOR RAMON
VS.
SHAWN MICHAELS

Razor Ramon and Shawn Michaels were both extremely talented in the ring and very popular with the WWE Universe. Their in-ring styles were similar—both possessed technical skills and a range of highly effective holds. Michaels liked to augment his holds with aerial moves, while Razor relied on sheer strength. When they competed against each other, fans were guaranteed excitement.

DID YOU KNOW?

Razor Ramon, under the name Scott Hall, founded the New World Order faction in 1996. Shawn Michaels joined the NWO in 2002.

"… I seen guys like you all my life, pampered boys who've never been slapped around. You gonna get slapped around, chico."

Maple Leaf Wrestling, August 21, 1993

1. Broken rules

RAW, September 27, 1993: Shawn Michaels had won the Intercontinental Championship on the May 17, 1993, episode of *RAW*. However, he didn't defend the Title as frequently as required by WWE rules (every 30 days), or even appear at WWE events, as mandated. So, WWE officials suspended Michaels and stripped him of the Championship, declaring that a new Intercontinental Champion would be crowned in the coming weeks.

2. Razor wins

RAW, October 11, 1993: A 20-Man Battle Royal was held on *RAW* with the stipulation that the final two Superstars in the match would compete against each other one-on-one the following week. The winner would become Intercontinental Champion. Ramon and Rick "The Model" Martel were the final two competitors. Razor used his Razor's Edge move to win the Title.

3. Double prize

WrestleMania X, March 20, 1994: Michaels returned from his suspension claiming that he had never lost the Intercontinental Championship. Current champ Ramon called Michaels a phony champ. The two competed in a Ladder Match, the first ever on pay-per-view, with both Intercontinental Titles hanging above the ring. Despite both men using the ladder in innovative ways, it was Ramon who stood tall, holding both titles at the end of the match.

RIVAL FACTS

- Razor Ramon won the Intercontinental Championship four times; Michaels won it three times.

- Michaels is a four-time WWE World Heavyweight Champion. Razor Ramon never won the Title.

- Shawn Michaels was inducted into the WWE Hall of Fame in 2011; Razor Ramon was inducted in 2014.

4. Pride at stake

RAW, August 1, 1994: By August, Ramon had lost his Intercontinental Championship, but he and Michaels still had unfinished business in the ring. In this match, both Superstars put their pride on the line. In the end, Michaels' bodyguard Diesel kicked Ramon, allowing Michaels to get a roll-up pin for the victory.

> **"I'm gonna say this slow so everyone can understand, especially Razor Ramon. I am the undisputed champion and you're not."**
>
> *Superstars,* December 4, 1993

THE KLIQ

Michaels and Ramon are both members of The Kliq, a group of Superstars who are also best friends. The Kliq includes "Diesel" Kevin Nash, X-Pac, and Triple H. Over the years, the Kliq teamed together and also competed against each other.

Action Zone (September 28, 1994) Tag Team Champions Michaels and Diesel defeated Ramon and X-Pac (then known as 1-2-3 Kid) in a Tag Team Title Match.

Curtain Call (May 19, 1996) Diesel and Ramon were leaving for rival company WCW. Following a match between Diesel and Michaels, Triple H and Ramon entered the ring. All four Superstars hugged, saying goodbye to their friends, and giving the Kliq's signature "Too Sweet" hand sign.

Hall of Fame (April 5, 2014) Following Ramon's Hall of Fame induction, all five members of the Kliq appeared on stage together for the first time since the Curtain Call.

RAW 25 (January 22, 2018) Ramon joined Triple H, Michaels, and X-Pac (who were members of D-Generation X) at the *RAW 25* spectacular, unofficially joining DX himself.

5. One more ladder

SummerSlam, August 27, 1995: Over a year after their legendary Ladder Match at *WrestleMania X*, Michaels and Ramon competed in another for the Intercontinental Championship. For the first time in WWE history, a second ladder was used. After a 30-minute struggle, Michaels climbed the ladder to win the Title. After the match, Ramon raised Michaels' hand in a show of respect.

"MACHO MAN" RANDY SAVAGE

VS.

"NATURE BOY" RIC FLAIR

Sixteen-time World Heavyweight Champion "Nature Boy" Ric Flair was known as "the dirtiest player in the game." He often cheated and he knew just how to psych out opponents, leading them to lose their cool and make crucial mistakes. When Flair started playing mind games with Randy Savage, Savage snapped and was determined to teach Flair a lesson.

1. Dirty tricks

***Superstars*, March 7, 1992:** Ric Flair was set to defend the WWE Championship against Randy Savage at *WrestleMania VIII*. To mess with Savage's head, Flair and his advisor, Mr. Perfect, revealed pictures that seemed to show Flair in a relationship with Savage's wife and manager, Elizabeth. Savage was furious, even though Flair claimed the pictures were taken before Elizabeth met Savage.

2. Savage's revenge

***WrestleMania VIII*, April 5, 1992:** Savage and Elizabeth proved the pictures were fake and had their chance to get back at Flair at *WrestleMania VIII*. Savage pummeled Flair throughout their match, and Elizabeth slapped Flair repeatedly for trying to harm her reputation. In the end, Flair was soundly defeated and Savage was crowned the new WWE Champion.

3. Two against one

SummerSlam, **August 19, 1992:**
Savage's first title defense was at *SummerSlam* against Ultimate Warrior, but an angry Ric Flair and Mr. Perfect weren't going to let that happen without a fight. They felt Flair was owed a rematch for the Title, and to prove the point, they interfered in the WWE Championship Match, attacking Savage and causing him to lose the match, but not the Title, by a countout.

> "Randy Savage, Elizabeth was mine before she was yours! Wooo!"
>
> *Superstars,* March 7, 1992

4. Championship rematch

Prime Time Wrestling, **September 14, 1992:**
When Flair got his rematch for the Championship, he made the most of his chance. Flair won by trapping Savage in his Figure-Four Leglock move. Savage refused to submit, despite the agony of the hold. He struggled for several minutes, trying to escape, finally passing out from the pain and resting his shoulders on the mat. The referee counted three and awarded the WWE Championship to Flair.

INTERNATIONAL BATTLES

Flair and Savage battled each other all over the world. Here are some of their biggest matches.

Philadelphia, Pennsylvania (August 2, 1992) Savage beat Flair with Superstar "Hacksaw" Jim Duggan as special referee.

Richfield, Ohio (September 12, 1992) Ric Flair defeated Randy Savage in a Steel Cage Match.

Hamburg, Germany (September 26, 1992) WWE Champion Flair defeated Savage to retain the Championship.

5. A Perfect partner

Survivor Series,
November 25, 1992: Savage was signed up for a tag team match against Flair and Razor Ramon at *Survivor Series*. With a week to go before the event, Savage didn't have a partner, so he did the unthinkable: he asked Flair's advisor, Mr. Perfect, to be his partner. Perfect, who had fallen out with Flair, accepted! The pair defeated Flair and Ramon by disqualification.

BRET "HIT MAN" HART VS. JERRY "THE KING" LAWLER

Jealousy can be a powerful motivator, and for Jerry "The King" Lawler, it's what pushed him into a rivalry with Bret "Hit Man" Hart. Hart liked to call himself the "Excellence of Execution" and "The best there is, the best there was, the best there ever will be!" Lawler disagreed, believing that *he* was the best ever. Lawler also thought Hart got more love from the WWE Universe when the fans should be bowing before "The King."

> **"Jerry Lawler, you are going to pay for every single thing you've ever said or done to myself or my family."**
> *Superstars,* October 17, 1993

1. Crown rivals

King of the Ring, **June 13, 1993:**
Bret "Hit Man" Hart won the annual King of the Ring tournament in 1993. During Hart's coronation, Jerry "The King" Lawler (who had used the nickname "The King" for many years) attacked Hart, declaring that he was the true king and Hart was an imposter. Lawler forced Hart to "kiss his foot" by kicking him.

2. Hail to The King!

SummerSlam, **August 30, 1993:**
For weeks, Lawler attacked Bret during his matches, beat his brother Owen, and insulted the brothers' parents: Stu and Helen Hart. Lawler and Hart's match at *SummerSlam* would decide who would have the right to call himself King of WWE. Bret held Lawler in a Sharpshooter hold and refused to let go. He was disqualified, handing Lawler the unofficial title of "King."

Jerry Lawler had a talk show segment called The King's Court, which he used to insult anyone connected to Bret Hart.

On Stu and Helen Hart (July 26, 1993) "I just wanted to come meet the people who produced more tragedies than Shakespeare."

On special guest, Owen Hart (July 18, 1993) "On the King's Court, I like to bring out a special guest. An individual of high integrity. An individual with a lot of talent and great ability. Somebody who's well loved and well respected by the fans. But unfortunately this week, my guest doesn't possess any of those qualities. Because my guest is the brother to the pretender to my throne Bret Hart—Owen Hart!"

3. Back for more

In Your House, May 14, 1995: Two years after their *SummerSlam* match, Bret and Lawler picked up where they'd left off. When Bret dedicated the match to his mother, Lawler mocked him by dedicating the match to his own "mother"—a younger model. Bret pinned Lawler, but the referee was knocked out of the ring and left hanging by his foot, unable to give the count. Lawler's friend Hakushi then attacked Bret, allowing Lawler to steal victory.

"Bret Hart, I am the only King of WWE!"

King of the Ring, June 13, 1993

4. Smell of defeat

King of the Ring, June 25, 1995: Returning to *King of the Ring,* where their rivalry began, Bret and Lawler competed in a Kiss My Foot Match, where the loser had to kiss the winner's foot. Bret forced Lawler to submit to his Sharpshooter move and then kiss his bare foot. Bret also made Lawler kiss his own sweaty, smelly foot!

5. Send for a dentist

SummerSlam, August 27, 1995: After kissing Bret's and his own foot, Lawler felt only his demented dentist, Dr. Isaac Yankem, could remove the taste of losing from his mouth. He also thought Yankem could finish off Hart once and for all. Although Lawler interfered throughout, Bret eventually overpowered Yankem to win the match, putting an end to Lawler's insults.

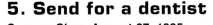

RIVAL FACTS

● Bret and Lawler are both WWE Hall of Fame inductees. Hart was inducted in 2006. Lawler was inducted in 2007 by *Star Trek* star William Shatner, a celebrity supporter of Bret Hart.

● Bret won every championship available during his time competing in WWE, while Jerry Lawler never won any WWE titles.

LEX LUGER
VS.
YOKOZUNA

"Yokozuna is a disgrace to WWE and we're going to clean house right here, right now!"

Yokozuna's Bodyslam Challenge, July 4, 1993

Yokozuna just could be the largest athlete to ever compete in WWE. At first sight, he seemed virtually unbeatable. He used his massive weight to crush opponents and win the WWE Championship. However, Lex Luger believed that he was strong enough to overcome Yokozuna's weight advantage. With his chiseled physique, Luger boasted that he, not Yokozuna, was WWE's most powerful Superstar.

275lbs (124.73kg)

1. Yokozuna's challenge

RAW, **July 5, 1993:** Filmed the day before, from the deck of the aircraft carrier U.S.S. *Intrepid*, Yokozuna issued a challenge. He dared WWE Superstars to try to bodyslam him. Several tried, but no one succeeded. Finally, a helicopter landed on the deck and Lex Luger jumped out. As Yokuzuna charged toward him, Luger hoisted Yokozuna up onto his shoulders and bodyslammed him, winning the challenge.

RIVAL FACTS

● Yokozuna was a two-time WWE Champion and two-time WWE Tag Team Champion. Luger never won a championship in WWE.

● Yokozuna was inducted into the WWE Hall of Fame in 2012. Luger has yet to receive that honor.

2. Luger's one shot

RAW, **August 9, 1993:** After slamming Yokozuna, Lex Luger sought a WWE Championship Match against the behemoth. Yokozuna refused, so Luger set out on a nationwide bus tour called the Lex Express to build fan support. The Lex Express campaign was successful, and Luger got the match. At the contract signing, Yokozuna's manager Jim Cornette revealed this would be Luger's only chance at the Title.

3. Counted out

SummerSlam, **August 30, 1993:** Luger's match for the Championship against Yokozuna came at *SummerSlam*. Luger hit Yokozuna with a running forearm that knocked Yokozuna out of the ring. Because of Yokozuna's massive weight, he was unable to get back in the ring by the end of the referee's count. As a result, he lost the match, but not the WWE Championship. Luger celebrated the victory, though he was disappointed not to win the Title.

4. Another chance

Royal Rumble, **January 22, 1994:** Luger desperately wanted another chance to face Yokozuna for the WWE Championship, but wasn't allowed to because of the original contract's stipulation. However, WWE officials said that if Luger could win the Royal Rumble Match against 29 other Superstars, he could have a Championship Match at *WrestleMania X*. After eliminating each other at the same moment, both Luger and Bret Hart were declared winners, and were each granted a *WrestleMania* match against Yokozuna.

589lbs (267.16kg)

> **"American athletes are just like American products. They are no good! Banzai!"**
>
> *RAW,* June 28, 1993

5. Yokozuna stands firm

WrestleMania X, **March 20, 1994:** Lex Luger faced Yokozuna early in the event, with the winner of their match facing Bret "Hit Man" Hart later in the night. Luger fought hard against Yokozuna, but wasn't gaining much of an advantage. Frustrated with what he felt were biased calls by special referee Mr. Perfect, Luger shoved Perfect, getting disqualified in the process. Luger lost the match and his final Championship opportunity.

BRET "HIT MAN" HART
VS.
OWEN HART

Growing up as one of the Hart family's 12 children, it could sometimes be hard to get parental attention. The best way to win it was to gain sports championships—particularly in amateur wrestling and sports entertainment. Arguably the most successful of Stu and Helen Hart's children was Bret "Hit Man" Hart. However, the Harts' youngest, Owen, resented Bret and set out to overshadow his brother's WWE accomplishments.

THE BREAKUP

> "Owen, sometimes you can't get what you want. Sometimes you get just what you need."
>
> *RAW*, March 21, 1994

1. Hart break
Bret Hart wanted to help build his brother Owen's WWE career. Owen resented this a bit, but joined Bret and their brothers Bruce and Keith against Shawn Michaels and three masked Superstars he called his knights in a *Survivor Series* Elimination Match. Owen was the only Hart eliminated in the match. He blamed Bret and attacked him after the match.

2. Brother vs. brother
***WrestleMania X**, March 20, 1994:* Bret tried to repair his relationship with Owen by partnering with him in a tag team match at *Royal Rumble*. However, Owen ended up attacking Bret. The brothers decided to settle their issues at *WrestleMania X*. In a back-and-forth contest, Owen pinned Bret for the win. Later that night, however, Owen looked on in disgust as Bret won the WWE Championship.

3. Caged in

SummerSlam, August 29, 1994:
Bret and Owen's hard feelings for each other escalated to the point where a Steel Cage Match seemed to be the only solution. Bret stuck Owen's legs in the frame of the cage and escaped it to win. Bret's victory celebration was rudely cut short when his brother-in-law Jim "The Anvil" Neidhart and Owen locked him inside the cage and beat him up.

4. Throwing the towel

Survivor Series, November 23, 1994:
Owen achieved his greatest victory over Bret in a match he wasn't even supposed to be in. Bret was defending his WWE Title against Bob Backlund in a Submission Match, in which the first Superstar whose towel was thrown into the ring would lose. Bret was caught in Backlund's Chicken Wing hold, but wouldn't give up. Owen tricked their mother, Helen, into throwing Bret's towel in the ring, costing him the match and WWE Championship.

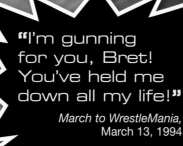

> **"I'm gunning for you, Bret! You've held me down all my life!"**
>
> *March to WrestleMania,*
> March 13, 1994

TAG TEAM RIVALS

Bret and Owen faced each other in several tag team matches. Here are four of their best.

RAW (November 7, 1994) Bret teamed with brother-in-law British Bulldog to defeat Owen and brother-in-law Jim Neidhart.

WWE Action Zone (January 25, 1995) Bret and British Bulldog defeated Owen and Bob Backlund.

RAW (March 3, 1995) Bret, Bob Holly, and 1-2-3 Kid beat the team of Owen, Hakushi, and Yokozuna.

Kuwait Cup (May 12, 1996) Bret and Undertaker defeated Owen and British Bulldog.

THE MAKEUP

5. The Hart Foundation

On the March 31, 1997 edition of *RAW*, Bret stepped in the middle of a fight between Owen and his brother-in-law British Bulldog. Bret pleaded with Owen and the Bulldog to remember the Hart family values and expressed his love for both Owen and the Bulldog. Owen embraced his brothers in a tearful hug, and all three soon became part of a new Hart Foundation faction.

ALUNDRA BLAYZE
VS.
BULL NAKANO

5ft 10in (1.78m)

Alundra Blayze had not reached the top of her game by merely relying on sheer strength and endurance. Instead, she'd used her in-ring technical expertise to win the WWE Women's Championship. But her next challenger was her toughest yet. Bull Nakano had only one desire: to become WWE Women's Champion by using her incredible strength and destroying everyone who got in her way. Blayze knew she'd have to work extra hard—physically and mentally—to overcome the driven Japanese Superstar who wanted her Title.

> **"Bull Nakano and I are on an even plateau. May the best woman win."**
>
> *All Japan Pro Wrestling,*
> November 20, 1994

1. Bull fighting

RAW, **August 1, 1994:** Alundra Blayze had defeated the best women WWE had to offer. One of Blayze's fallen opponents, Luna Vachon, introduced a new opponent for Blayze from Japan—Bull Nakano. Blayze faced Nakano in a non-title match that saw the action spill outside the ring. Both women got so distracted by battling each other, they didn't hear the referee's count and were counted out.

2. Title grab

SummerSlam, **August 29, 1994:** As a result of her strong showing against Blayze on *RAW*, Nakano was granted a Women's Championship Match at *SummerSlam*. Nakano used her weight advantage to try to crush Blayze. Blayze countered with aerial moves that took down her heavier opponent. Nakano's manager, Luna Vachon, attacked Blayze behind the referee's back, but it didn't help her client. Blayze pinned Nakano to retain the WWE Women's Championship.

5ft 7in
(1.70m)

3. Double up

RAW, October 3, 1994: Luna Vachon and Nakano were determined to defeat Blayze by working together. Blayze found a tag team partner in Heidi Lee Morgan to help her fend off the rival pair. Their tag team match ended when Vachon accidentally kicked Nakano while flying off the top rope. Blayze capitalized on the blunder with a pin to secure the victory.

4. Nakano's time

All Japan Women's Pro Wrestling,
November 20, 1994: In a very special event presented by All Japan Pro Wrestling inside the Tokyo Dome, Blayze defended the WWE Women's Championship against Nakano. In front of a home crowd of approximately 40,000 supporters, Nakano hit Blayze with a legdrop off the top rope, pinning her rival, and finally winning the Championship she had so long desired.

WCW RESTART

Blayze and Nakano's rivalry extended from WWE into rival sports entertainment company World Championship Wrestling (WCW), where they faced each other twice.

Hog Wild (August 10, 1996) After pinning Nakano for the win, Blayze was allowed to destroy Nakano's Japanese motorcycle as the result of a prematch stipulation. The event was being held in front of the largest American motorcycle rally in Sturgis, South Dakota.

Clash of the Champions (August 15, 1996) Blayze pinned Nakano for the three count after Nakano was accidentally kicked by her own manager, Sonny Ohno.

5. Blayzing Bull

RAW, April 3, 1995: Nearly six months after their showdown in Japan, it was Nakano's turn to defend the WWE Women's Championship against Blayze. Nakano went to the top rope and attempted a back-flipping moonsault onto Blayze, but Blayze moved. In a display of amazing strength, Blayze picked up Nakano and threw her backward in a belly-to-back-suplex pin to regain the Championship.

BOB BACKLUND VS. BRET "HIT MAN" HART

Bret "Hit Man" Hart and Bob Backlund were from different generations of sports entertainment, but were similar in many ways. Both were amateur wrestling champions who brought their exceptional mat skills with them to WWE and became champions. But when the old champion, Backlund, came back to the ring to settle scores and take on the current champion, Hart, an epic battle of the eras began.

"Bret Hart is part of a society that I have nothing to do with. They're not disciplined enough. They don't work hard enough. And they don't pay the price."

RAW, August 1, 1994

1. The old vs. the new

***Superstars*, July 30, 1994:**
Bob Backlund was a WWE Champion in the late 1970s. He returned to WWE in the 1990s hoping to once again become champion. To prove himself, Backlund faced current WWE Champion Bret Hart in a match for the Title called "Old Generation vs. New Generation." Backlund pinned Hart and thought he had won the Title, but he was wrong. Hart surprised Backlund by rolling him up for a pin and win.

2. Court appearance

***RAW*, August 1, 1994:** Backlund appeared on Jerry Lawler's King Court declaring that he had never truly lost the WWE Championship in the 1970s. He claimed he'd never submitted, but that his manager Arnold Skaaland had thrown his towel into the ring, quitting on Backlund's behalf. Backlund insulted Hart and swore he'd defeat him for the Title.

> "You have this dream about being the WWE Champion? It's not going to happen, Bob."
>
> *Superstars*, November 5, 1994

3. Mother's nature

Survivor Series, **November 23, 1994:** Backlund challenged Hart to a Submission Match, where the only way to win was have your opponent's corner man throw the towel in. Backlund's corner man, Bret's estranged brother, Owen, and Bret's corner man, British Bulldog, ended up fighting, allowing Backlund to trap Bret in his Chicken Wing submission hold for eight minutes. Hart's mother Helen couldn't bear seeing her son suffer and threw the towel in, giving Backlund the WWE Championship he'd craved for so long.

4. Interference

Royal Rumble, **January 22, 1995:** Backlund won the WWE Championship from Hart. Three days later, he lost it to Diesel in just eight seconds. Diesel gave a Title match to Bret at the *Royal Rumble* shortly after. Enraged, Backlund and Bret's brother Owen interfered with the match, attacking Bret, and costing him his chance at regaining the Championship.

5. I quit!

WrestleMania XI, **April 2, 1995:** Backlund and Bret next battled at *WrestleMania XI* where they faced each other in an "I Quit Match." Hart locked his Sharpshooter hold on Backlund and special referee "Rowdy" Roddy Piper placed the microphone next to Backlund's mouth. Backlund spoke some indecipherable gibberish that Piper interpreted as "I quit," and awarded the match to Bret. Following the loss, Backlund retired from in-ring competition and became a manager for other WWE Superstars.

RIVAL FACTS

- Hart won seven World Championships in his career; Backlund won two. Backlund's two WWE Championship wins were 16 years apart.

- Both Superstars were inducted into the WWE Hall of Fame—Backlund in 2013, Hart in 2006.

DIESEL VS. SHAWN MICHAELS

After splitting from his longtime tag team partner Marty Jannetty, Shawn Michaels was looking for someone to replace him. Michaels hired Diesel as his bodyguard, bringing him into WWE and forming a new tag team partnership. Diesel and Michaels were close partners until they began competing for the same WWE Championships. These on-again, off-again partners knew each other so well that it was always a big battle when they met in the ring.

THE BREAKUP

1. Team divided

Shawn Michaels and Diesel were riding on the back of victories: Together they held the Tag Team Titles and Diesel was also the current Intercontinental Champion. But at 1994's *Survivor Series*, Michaels accidentally kicked Diesel and cost him his individual Championship Title. The duo angrily split and Michaels soon hired a new bodyguard in the form of Sycho Sid, who was the same size as Diesel.

2. New allegiances

***WrestleMania XI*, April 2, 1995:** Diesel had won the WWE Championship and now had to defend it against Michaels, who had earned the match by winning a 30-Man Royal Rumble Match. With new bodyguard Sid ringside, Michaels fought hard for the Title, but Sid mistakenly distracted the referee when Michaels had Diesel pinned. Diesel fought back and defeated his former partner to retain the WWE Championship.

3. Back together?

In Your House: Triple Header, **September 24, 1995:** Briefly improving their relationship as they shared a mutual championship goal, Michaels and Diesel reformed their tag team following *WrestleMania XI.* They called themselves The Dudes With Attitudes and competed for the Tag Team Championship against Champions Owen Hart and Yokozuna. When they pinned Owen Hart, they became Tag Team Champions, but days later, the decision was reversed and the team split once again.

4. Keep your enemies close

In Your House: Good Friends, Better Enemies, **April 28, 1996:** Michaels had recently won the WWE Championship from Bret "Hit Man" Hart at *WrestleMania XII,* and Diesel wanted to grasp the biggest Title in WWE from his former friend. The Superstars ferociously fought it out in a No Holds Barred Match. They used chairs, tables, low blows, and other ruthless attacks—including using a false leg as a weapon—before Michaels hit Diesel with a superkick, and pinned him for the win.

DID YOU KNOW?

Shawn Michaels inducted Diesel, under the name Kevin Nash, into the WWE Hall of Fame.

"Diesel, when I cue up the music and hit you with Sweet Chin Music, you'll have no choice but to go straight down!"

Superstars, May 18, 1996

RIVAL FACTS

● Diesel was a recognized World Heavyweight Champion on five occasions; Shawn Michaels received four World Championships in his career.

● Michaels won six Tag Team Championships in WWE; Diesel won the Tag Team Championship twice—both times with Michaels.

● Michaels held the Intercontinental Championship three times; Diesel held it once.

THE MAKEUP

5. Dudes reunited

After the No Holds Barred Match, Diesel left WWE for rival company WCW. A year later, Michaels also left the company. Both men returned in 2002. Diesel reformed his WCW faction the nWo, which Michaels joined. Together again, the pair faced teams like Evolution and remained friends from then on.

ATTITUDE ERA

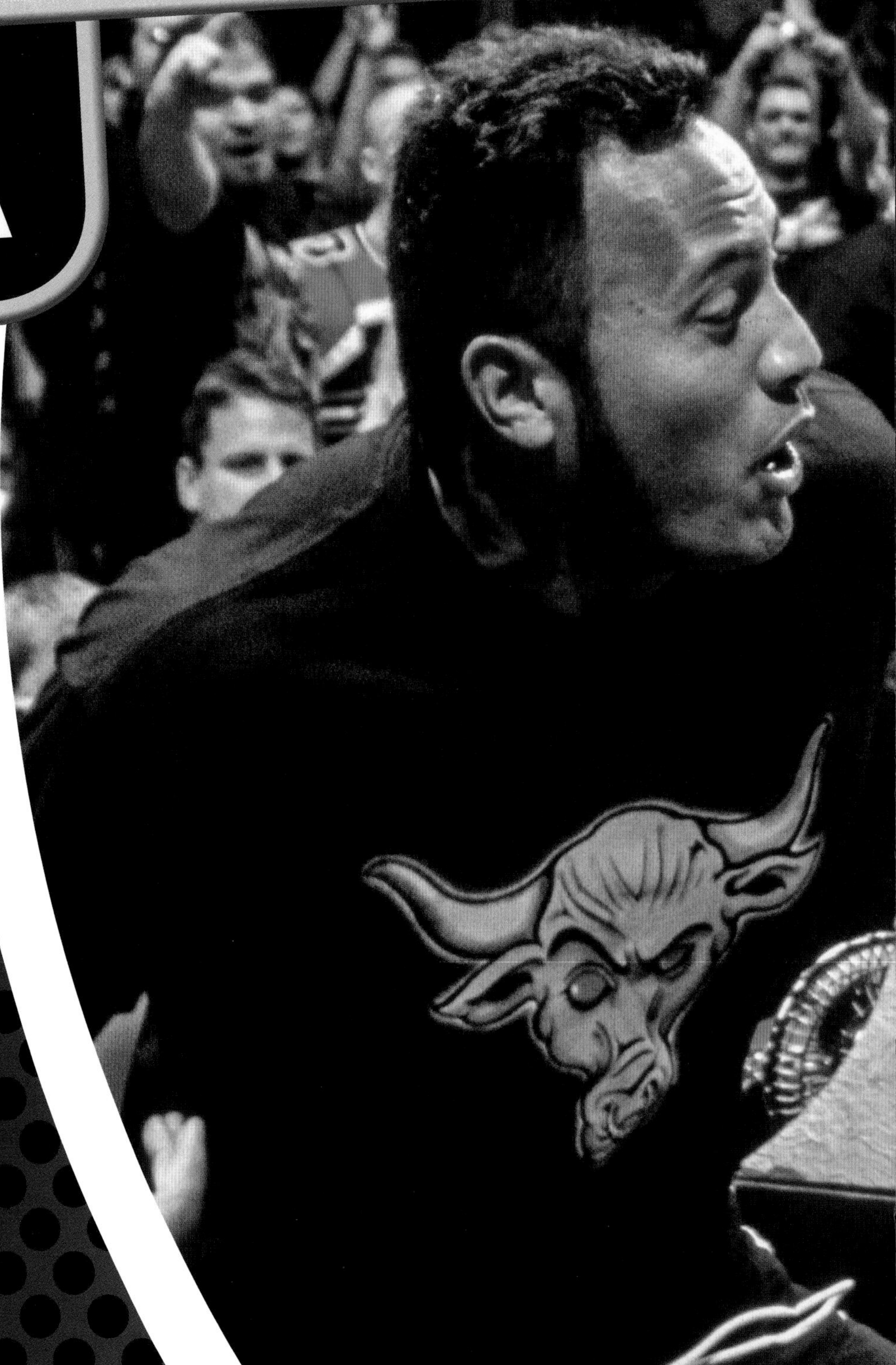

BRET "HIT MAN" HART

vs.

SHAWN MICHAELS

Considering their rivalry, Bret "Hit Man" Hart and Shawn Michaels had much in common. Roughly the same size, the pair were both in-ring technical wizards, had started as members of a popular tag team, and competed for the same titles at the same time. These close similarities led to a competitive rivalry that started out strictly professional, but was destined to end on the most personal of terms.

THE BREAKUP

1. The same path

In the early 1990s, Hart and Michaels both left their tag teams (The Hart Foundation and The Rockers respectively) to pursue singles titles. They both initially set out to win the Intercontinental Championship, then the WWE Championship. Hart would be first to secure both of these Titles, but the pair battled each other several times in attempts to prove superiority over the other.

6ft (1.82m)

2. The first war

Survivor Series, **November 25, 1992:** It was a battle of champions: Hart had recently won the WWE Championship from Ric Flair, while Michaels was the current Intercontinental Champion. For this match, however, only Hart's Title was on the line. The pair matched each other move for move, but Hart was eventually able to force Michaels to submit to his Sharpshooter finishing hold and retain his Title.

- Hart won seven World Heavyweight Championships in his career; Shawn Michaels won four.

- Hart is a two-time Intercontinental Champion, while Michaels held that Title three times.

- Michaels held the Tag Team Championship six times; Hart was a two-time Tag Team Champion.

- Both Superstars have been inducted into the WWE Hall of Fame—Hart in 2006, Michaels in 2011.

3. Dreams come true

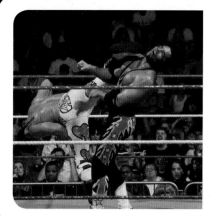

WrestleMania XII, March 31, 1996: Michaels' boyhood dream of becoming WWE Champion came true at *WrestleMania XII* when he faced Hart in a 60-minute Iron Match, where the Superstar who won the most falls won the match. After an hour of intense back-and-forth competition, neither man had won a fall. In sudden death overtime, Michaels hit Hart with his Sweet Chin Music move and pinned Hart to win the Championship.

6ft 1in (1.85m)

4. The Montreal Screwjob

Survivor Series, November 9, 1997: Hart and Michaels entered *Survivor Series* in 1997 with a bitter new edge to their rivalry. Hart had called out Michaels' profanity, vulgar jokes, and inappropriate behavior as an embarrassment, while Michaels suspected Hart of having an affair with his girlfriend. Further heightening emotions, Hart had decided to leave WWE for rival company WCW. As Michaels applied Hart's own finishing move against his rival, WWE Chairman Mr. McMahon ordered the referee to ring the bell and award the Title to Michaels—cheating Hart of the Championship.

DID YOU KNOW?

Bret and Shawn had the very first Ladder Match in WWE for the Intercontinental Championship on *Wrestling Challenge* (July 21, 1992).

THE MAKEUP

5. Burying the hatchet

The January 10, 2010 episode of *RAW* saw Hart return to WWE for the first time in more than 12 years and since the controversial night of the Montreal Screwjob. Hart called out Michaels, looking to settle their old issues. The pair both expressed regret for their actions and Hart extended his hand in friendship. Michaels shook Hart's hand and the two Superstars shared a hug.

> **"I've beaten you. I've beaten your brother. I've beaten your brothers-in-law, and I'll beat up your whole family if you get in my face one more time."**
>
> *RAW*, October 13, 1997

WCW VS. WWE

When Vince McMahon took over WWE in 1982, he began buying the rest of the brands out, building WWE into a massive national brand. Only one sports entertainment brand remained—World Championship Wrestling (WCW), owned by billionaire Ted Turner. Turner sought to make WCW a national brand, like WWE. But to do that, he'd have to put WWE out of business ....

1. Going to war on a Monday

Ted Turner launched a new show to air directly opposite WWE's *Monday Night RAW*. WCW's *Monday Nitro* premiered on September 4, 1995. WCW President Eric Bischoff lured some of WWE's biggest names, such as Hulk Hogan, Randy "Macho Man" Savage, Scott Hall (known in WWE as Razor Ramon), and Kevin Nash (WWE's Diesel) from WWE to WCW with the promise of huge paychecks.

Bischoff stirred up trouble by giving away the results of taped WWE matches and arranged for WWE Women's Champion Alundra Blayze to dump her Title in the garbage live on *Nitro*. Turner created the rebellious nWo faction, introduced new stars such as Sting, Goldberg, and Diamond Dallas Page, and aired matches usually reserved for pay-per-view on regular television. WCW then launched another weekly prime-time show, *WCW Thunder,* in January 1998. Suddenly, WCW was challenging WWE for power.

2. Back with Attitude

WWE had been a family-friendly show, but with new competition from WCW, WWE changed course and the more adult-oriented "Attitude Era" commenced. The action became controversial, and Stone Cold Steve Austin, The Rock, D-Generation X, Mankind, and Undertaker became WWE's biggest stars.

As *RAW* became fresh and exciting, *Nitro* became repetitive in its storytelling. Viewers switched from WCW to WWE in droves. Superstars such as Chris Jericho, Big Show, and X-Pac left WCW for WWE's higher-profile matches and championship opportunities. WWE had turned around its fortunes and overtaken WCW in popularity. WWE then launched *SmackDown* to air opposite *WCW Thunder* on Thursday April 29, 1999. WWE was once again firmly in control of sports entertainment.

DID YOU KNOW?

On the January 4, 1999, edition of *Nitro*, WCW Announcer Tony Schiavone revealed that Mick Foley would win the WWE Championship on *RAW*. Unfortunately, more than half a million viewers then switched over to *RAW*!

3. Owning the competition

Keen to compete against his father, WWE Chairman Vince McMahon, Shane McMahon swooped in and bought WCW. In the weeks following his WCW purchase, Shane warned WWE that his WCW Superstars would take over WWE. A pay-per-view event called *Invasion* on July 22, 2001 featured matches between Superstars from WWE and WCW (and its new ally ECW, now owned by Stephanie McMahon). At *Survivor Series* that year, Vince's Team WWE defeated their WCW/ECW counterparts representing Shane and Stephanie. This forced the WCW/ECW Alliance to dissolve.

When Chris Jericho won both the WWE and WCW Championships at the December 2001 *Vengeance* pay-per-view by beating The Rock and Stone Cold Steve Austin, the two Titles were unified into one Title, named the WWE Undisputed Championship. This effectively dissolved WCW. An epic era of sports entertainment was gone forever, with WWE standing tall, the ultimate victor.

THE ROCK VS. TRIPLE H

These two titans of sports entertainment entered WWE in the same year, 1996, and climbed the ladder of success rung by rung at the same time. They competed for the Intercontinental Championship and then the WWE Championship. Triple H led the D-Generation X faction, while The Rock headed the Nation of Domination. Whenever their paths crossed, the results were explosive.

THE BREAKUP

DID YOU KNOW?

Triple H once impersonated The Rock, calling himself The Crock, angering The Rock and his Nation of Domination teammates.

1. From day one

Their rivalry began in The Rock's very first match. Debuting at *Survivor Series* (1996) as part of an eight-man Elimination Match, The Rock (then known as Rocky Maivia) was the sole survivor, defeating the other four-person team, which included Triple H (then known as Hunter Hearst Helmsley). From that moment on, The Rock and Triple H were prime adversaries.

2. Surprise pin

RAW, **February 13, 1997:** On a special Thursday night edition of *RAW*, Triple H and The Rock had their first match for the Intercontinental Championship. It looked as though Triple H would come out on top, retaining his Championship. However, while Triple H was posing in the ring, The Rock rolled him up in a surprise pin to win the Championship.

3. Escaping the cage

Rebellion, October 2, 1999: The rivalry between Triple H and The Rock had grown personal, with insults, sneak attacks, and match-costing interference. Triple H had become WWE Champion and he defended his Title in a Steel Cage Match at the *Rebellion* pay-per-view, in Birmingham, England. Triple H's bodyguard, Chyna, slammed the cage door on The Rock, allowing Triple H to escape and retain the Championship.

RIVAL FACTS

● Triple H has won the Royal Rumble Match twice (2002, 2016) while The Rock has won it once (2000).

● Triple H is a 14-time WWE Champion; The Rock is a 10-time WWE Champion.

● The Rock has held the WWE Tag Team Championship on five occasions; Triple H has held it three times.

● Triple H and The Rock have both been multi-time Intercontinental Champions: Triple H five times, and The Rock twice.

● Triple H is a former *King of the Ring* winner. The Rock has never won that tournament.

4. No winner yet

RAW, August 19, 2002: The final match between Triple H and The Rock was a No Disqualification Match. The Rock was WWE Champion, but this match was only for honor. The match ended in a no-contest draw when Triple H brought out a hammer and Brock Lesnar and Shawn Michaels jumped into the ring. The WWE Universe was left to wonder whether Triple H or The Rock was the superior Superstar.

"I have nothing to prove to you!"
WrestleMania 31, March 29, 2015

THE MAKEUP

5. It never ends

At *WrestleMania 31*, more than 12 years since their last match, Triple H and The Rock once again faced off in the ring when The Rock and his friend Ronda Rousey interrupted Triple H and his wife Stephanie McMahon, who were boasting about their success in the ring. Before long, the war of words turned into a full-on brawl, with The Rock and Triple H once again trading blows.

TRIPLE THREAT MATCHES

While The Rock and Triple H faced each other many times one-on-one, many of their matches for the WWE Championship were Triple Threat Matches, which included a third Superstar inserting himself into their rivalry.

RAW (March 20, 2000) Triple H faced The Rock and Big Show in the main event, defeating both Superstars, and remaining WWE Champion.

Insurrextion (May 6, 2000) In London, England, The Rock successfully defended the WWE Championship against Shane McMahon and Triple H.

SummerSlam (August 27, 2000) The Rock defeated both Triple H and Kurt Angle to hold onto the WWE Championship.

Global Warming (August 10, 2002) WWE Champion The Rock successfully defended the Title against Triple H and Brock Lesnar in Melbourne, Australia.

MANKIND
VS.
UNDERTAKER

Both these Superstars lurk in the shadows and find comfort in darkness and evil. They are willing to endure unimaginable pain to win and are known for inflicting even worse pain on their opponents. Despite their similar natures, Mankind and Undertaker reviled each other. Mankind was particularly jealous of Undertaker's mastery of the dark side and the adulation he received from the WWE Universe.

THE BREAKUP

DID YOU KNOW?
At different times in their rivalry, both Superstars were managed by Paul Bearer.

1. Dark times
At the *RAW* after *WrestleMania XII* (April 1, 1996), Mankind sat alone in a boiler room, petting rats and plotting to inflict harm on a society that he felt had rejected him. In his twisted mind, Mankind believed Undertaker represented this backstabbing society, and began interfering in Undertaker's matches. Soon, Undertaker returned the favor, and a dark, twisted rivalry was born.

2. Boiling point
SummerSlam, **August 18, 1996:** After months of taunting and violent confrontation, Mankind and Undertaker met in the first ever "Boiler Room Brawl." The object of this match was to escape the arena's boiler room and race to the ring to retrieve Undertaker's urn from Paul Bearer. Although Undertaker was the first to reach the ring, he was unable to claim the urn, resulting in Mankind securing the victory.

3. Buried alive!

In Your House: Buried Alive,
October 20, 1996: Having competed in a bizarre match designed by Mankind at *SummerSlam*, the Superstars faced each other in an equally twisted one created by Undertaker at *In Your House: Buried Alive*. Undertaker's Buried Alive Match required the winner to drive their opponent into a shallow grave and cover them with dirt. As the inventor of the match, it was no surprise when Undertaker won, burying Mankind "six feet under."

4. A long way down

***King of the Ring*, June 28, 1998:** It would become the match type most synonymous with their rivalry: Undertaker and Mankind in the giant Hell in a Cell steel cage. At one point, they fought on top of the cage and Undertaker threw Mankind 20 feet (6.1m) off the top, sending him crashing through the ringside commentators' table. Later in the match, Undertaker slammed Mankind through the cage's ceiling to the ring. It was a win for Undertaker, but a victory of sorts for Mankind in that he survived to fight again.

NO HOLDS BARRED

Undertaker and Mankind had several "No Holds Barred" matches with no set rules and no limits.

In Your House: Revenge of the Taker (April 20, 1997) Undertaker threw balls of fire at Mankind and his former manager Paul Bearer, and used his signature Tombstone Pile Driver to defeat Mankind and retain the Championship.

RAW (February 3, 1997) Undertaker and Ahmed Johnson took the No Holds Barred challenge of Mankind and Faarooq. Thanks to steel chairs, interference from Vader, and a Tombstone Piledriver, Undertaker and Johnson's team won.

RAW (September 14, 1999) Mankind brought a garbage dumpster full of weapons, including The Rock, who interfered on Mankind's behalf, causing a no-contest draw.

> "Mankind, I never forgive and I never forget."
>
> *RAW*, August 18, 1997

THE MAKEUP

5. Back to the shadows

Undertaker and Mankind continued to battle each other throughout the rest of the 1990s, but their rivalry was never more intense than it had been in their Hell in a Cell Match. They grew to begrudgingly respect each other, though they were never friends. Nevertheless, their brutal matches resulted in their names being etched in sports entertainment history.

RIVAL FACTS

● Undertaker is a seven-time WWE Champion; Mankind is a three-time Champion.

● Both Undertaker and Mankind won the Tag Team Championship with Stone Cold Steve Austin, Kane, and The Rock as partners, but never together.

THE HART FOUNDATION
VS.
STONE COLD STEVE AUSTIN

Bret "Hit Man" Hart had taken time away from WWE. While he was gone, Stone Cold Steve Austin's rebellious attitude helped him rise in popularity. Bret returned and made it clear how disgusted he was by Austin's attitude. Bret reformed The Hart Foundation—a faction made up of members of the Hart family from Calgary, Canada. The Foundation believed Austin represented everything that was wrong with America and wanted to punish him.

> **"Stone Cold Steve Austin is in for the worst thrashing of his entire life!"**
> —Bret Hart *RAW*, March 17, 1997

1. No surrender
***WrestleMania 13*, March 23, 1997:** They had been ruining each other's matches and chances at the WWE Championship for weeks. Then Bret and Austin faced each other in a Submission Match, where they had to try to force the other to submit. After a brutal back-and-forth slugfest, Bret put Austin in his Sharpshooter finishing move. Austin refused to give up, but passed out from the pain, making Bret the winner.

2. Five against one
RAW, **June 9, 1997:** The five members of The Hart Foundation challenged any five American Superstars to a match at the upcoming *Canadian Stampede* pay-per-view. Austin was the first Superstar to accept the challenge— leading to a five-on-one attack by The Foundation. Austin tried his best, but the odds were too much for him.

3. It's a family affair

In Your House: Canadian Stampede, **July 6, 1997:** At the famous Calgary Stampede rodeo, The Hart Foundation faced Austin, Ken Shamrock, Goldust, and the Legion of Doom. Many members of the large Hart family sat ringside and took cheap shots at the American team—especially Austin. Following a multiple-Hart beatdown on Austin, Owen Hart rolled Austin up for the pin.

4. A unique challenge

RAW, **July 7, 1997:** The night after *Canadian Stampede*, The Hart Foundation celebrated their victory by singing Canada's national anthem in the ring. Austin attacked the Foundation in the middle of the song, specifically targeting Owen. Later in the evening, Austin challenged Owen to a match for Owen's Intercontinental Championship at *SummerSlam* the next month, promising that if he didn't win the Title, Austin would literally kiss Owen's rear end!

> "The bottom line is, when Stone Cold's in the house, Bret Hart's at his house, because he's scared of Stone Cold."
>
> *In Your House: Mind Games*,
> September 22, 1996

BATTLES FOR THE TITLE

Austin battled The Hart Foundation in several other matches ....

In Your House: Revenge of the Taker (April 20, 1997) Austin and Bret Hart competed to be Number One Contender for the WWE Championship. Austin won by disqualification, after an attack by The Foundation.

RAW (May 26, 1997) WWE President Gorilla Monsoon ordered Steve Austin to team with Shawn Michaels to take on WWE Tag Team Champions British Bulldog and Owen Hart. Austin and Michaels won the fast-paced match and the Titles.

RAW (July 21, 1997) In their home country of Canada, Bret, Owen, and British Bulldog competed in a Flag Match against Austin, Dude Love, and Undertaker. Thanks to help from Foundation member Brian Pillman, Bret Hart captured the Canadian flag and won the match.

5. The end

SummerSlam, **August 3, 1997:** Owen accepted Austin's challenge, and a brawl ensued at WWE's biggest summertime event. Owen used his best technical in-ring skills while Austin pummeled his opponent with punches and kicks. In the end, Austin, despite being severely injured, rolled up Owen for the pin to win the Intercontinental Championship. Within a couple of months, The Hart Foundation disbanded, while Austin recovered from his serious injury.

ECW
VS.
WWE

Launched in 1993, Extreme Championship Wrestling (ECW) was owned and run by former WCW personality Paul Heyman. It soon became known for its extremely violent matches and its loyal fanbase. By 1996, ECW had grown into a national sports entertainment brand, one big enough, and hungry enough, to challenge WWE's supremacy. To grab the world's attention, ECW decided to attack the WWE Superstars in their own backyard!

1. The ECW invasion

On September 22, 1996, ECW Superstars, including Tommy Dreamer, Tazz, The Sandman, and Paul Heyman, bought tickets to WWE's *Mind Games* pay-per-view event. They were kicked out of the arena, but the stunt worked. Fans started bringing ECW signs and t-shirts to WWE events. Annoyed, WWE announcer Jerry Lawler challenged ECW (dubbing it "Extremely Crappy Wrestling") to bring its Superstars to the February 24, 1997, episode of *RAW*. ECW gleefully obliged.

A few months later, Lawler showed up at a June 7, 1997, ECW pay-per-view event and attacked Tommy Dreamer. The war between ECW and WWE was on, with Superstars from both sides competing on each others' shows for the following months.

2. WWE comes out on top

Exposure via WWE brought ECW increased popularity. It gained national pay-per-view events, action figures, video games, and even a show on cable TV. However, ECW did not have the financial resources to sustain such success. WWE and WCW both promised more money and fame, and several ECW Superstars soon left for greener pastures. WWE's *RAW* replaced ECW's show and ECW's creative force, Paul Heyman, became a *RAW* announcer.

ECW went bankrupt and, on the July 9, 2001 episode of *SmackDown*, Stephanie McMahon declared that she had bought the company. She aligned ECW with her brother Shane's WCW to form the Alliance (pictured right), a faction of Superstars that wanted to put an end to WWE. By the end of 2001, however, the Alliance had folded. WWE stood supreme in sports entertainment, and the brand name ECW seemed dead and gone.

DID YOU KNOW?

Rob Van Dam was the only Superstar to have been both ECW Champion and WWE Champion simultaneously.

3. A brief revival

ECW was gone, but not forgotten. On June 12, 2005, WWE produced an ECW reunion pay-per-view called *One Night Stand*, featuring former ECW Superstars. Some WWE Superstars resented the revival, and like their ECW counterparts nearly a decade before, staged an invasion. The show ended in a huge brawl, with Team ECW emerging as victors and celebrating in fine style.

A year later, a second *One Night Stand* show was held, heralding a new weekly ECW television show under the WWE banner. This debuted on June 13, 2006, and featured a mix of ECW originals and lesser-known WWE Superstars. Not as "extreme" as the original ECW show, it became a place for WWE rookies to learn their craft. By February 16, 2010, however, ECW was replaced by WWE NXT.

MANKIND

VS.

TRIPLE H

Triple H and Mankind both entered WWE in 1996, and were at odds from the start. Triple H, then known as the aristocratic Hunter Hearst Helmsley, thought Mankind was a freak. Mankind resented Triple H's wealth and power. Their hatred for each other led them to invent new violent ways to decimate one another, regardless of whether any titles were on the line.

"As much as I've dreamed about destroying Hunter Hearst Helmsley ... I know someone who dreams about it even more ... Cactus Jack is back"

RAW, September 22, 1997

1. Royal blues
***King of the Ring,* June 8, 1997:** Mankind and Triple H found themselves in the finals of the King of the Ring tournament. Thanks to help from his bodyguard Chyna, Triple H outlasted Mankind and won the tournament. Triple H's disgust for Mankind surfaced, however; he smashed Mankind with his newly won crown.

2. Caged in
***SummerSlam,* August 3, 1997:** The animosity between Mankind and Triple H continued to grow in intensity. After attacking each other during matches and outside the ring, they battled inside a steel cage. Mankind put himself at extreme risk to dive off the top of the cage onto Triple H, and escaped it first to win the match.

Mankind created Boiler Room Brawl Matches to face Undertaker, but he also faced Triple H in two heated matches.

SmackDown (September 23, 1999) Triple H escaped the boiler room first, winning the match and advancing to a WWE Championship Six Pack Challenge Match at the *Unforgiven* pay-per-view.

RAW (December 20, 1999) Mick Foley was forced into a boiler room for a match against "Santa Claus." After multiple Superstars disguised as Santa Claus beat down Foley, Triple H—also in a Santa outfit — escaped the boiler room for the win.

3. Here's Cactus Jack!

RAW, **September 22, 1997:** Triple H sought revenge on Mankind—and this included Mankind's alter-ego, Dude Love, a hippy persona created in the fractured mind of Mankind's true self, Mick Foley. Triple H challenged Dude Love to a Falls Count Anywhere Match in Madison Square Garden. Both Mankind and Dude Love rejected the challenge, but a third persona, Cactus Jack, a Superstar who loved ultra-violent matches, accepted and defeated Triple H in a brutal match.

4. Champ for a day

RAW, **August 23, 1999:** The night after *SummerSlam*, where Mankind had defeated Triple H and Stone Cold Steve Austin to win his first WWE Championship, Triple H challenged Mankind to a Title defense. With his friend Shane McMahon as special referee, Triple H used his Pedigree finisher on Mankind to strip Mankind of the Title he'd held for just one day.

5. Mankind lives on

No Way Out, **February 27, 2000:** The battle between Mankind and Triple H reached its conclusion inside the confines of another steel cage. WWE Champion Triple H put his Title on the line against Mankind's career. Desperate to continue in WWE, Mankind cheated the system by entering the match as Cactus Jack. It was Jack who fought valiantly, but lost the match and retired from full-time in-ring competition.

"Mick Foley ... I will beat you worse than you have ever been beaten in your entire life!"

SmackDown, January 13, 2000

RIVAL FACTS

● Triple H is a 14-time WWE World Heavyweight Champion; Mankind is a three-time champ.

● Triple H defeated Mankind to win both the King of the Ring Tournament and his first WWE Championship.

● Both Mankind and Triple H have served as authority figures on *RAW*.

THE ROCK
VS.
STONE COLD STEVE AUSTIN

The Rock and Stone Cold Steve Austin, two of the most popular WWE Superstars of all time, had one of the most intense and longest rivalries. Both Superstars were driven to be number one and realized that the other stood in his way. Nothing was going to stop either Superstar from claiming the top spot in the company, so they battled each other for the WWE Championship on countless occasions on *RAW*, *SmackDown*, and at *WrestleMania*.

THE BREAKUP

> "Do you have what it takes to go one on one against 'The Great One'?"
>
> *RAW*, March 3, 2003

1. First clash

It had been less than a year since The Rock had debuted in WWE, but he had fought hard to rise through the ranks to compete for the WWE Intercontinental Championship, held by Stone Cold Steve Austin. Their first in-ring encounter was a short but intense match at *In Your House: D-Generation X* (December 7, 1997) that Austin won, retaining the Title.

2. Disqualification ploy

RAW, **November 16, 1998:** WWE Champion The Rock had joined forces with Mr. McMahon's evil Corporation stable. The Corporation's number one goal was ending Austin's career. But when Austin revealed that he had a contract giving him the first match for The Rock's Title, The Rock was forced to defend against him. Austin nearly had the Championship won; however, outside interference by Undertaker resulted in Austin only winning by disqualification, thus not gaining the Championship.

3. The heat is on

WrestleMania XV, March 28, 1999: The rivalry between The Rock and Austin had grown white hot. At *WrestleMania XV*, they battled for the WWE Championship, held by The Rock. It was the first of three times they would compete in the headlining match at a *WrestleMania* event. Following a hard-fought battle, Austin emerged victorious, winning his third WWE Championship.

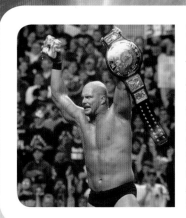

4. A shock alliance

WrestleMania X-Seven, April 1, 2001: Austin had won the 2001 Royal Rumble Match, earning him a match against WWE Champion The Rock at *WrestleMania*. It was a No Disqualification Match, and the WWE Universe was shocked when Austin joined forces with his most hated adversary, Mr. McMahon. He gave Austin a steel chair to use against The Rock, which he took advantage of to win the Championship.

WWE CHAMPIONSHIP BOUTS

Outside of their epic *WrestleMania* battles, The Rock and Austin faced each other for the WWE Championship in several memorable matches.

Backlash (April 25, 1999) A No Disqualification Match with The Rock's Corporation colleague Shane McMahon as special referee. Winner: Austin

RAW (May 2, 1999) A rare Lumberjack Match, in which countless WWE Superstars surrounded the ring and attacked The Rock and Austin. Winner: None (no-contest draw)

RAW (April 2, 2001) The night after *WrestleMania X-Seven*, The Rock and Austin faced off in a *WrestleMania* rematch, this time inside a steel cage. Winner: None (no-contest draw)

Rebellion (November 3, 2001) A special pay-per-view event held in England. Winner: Austin

THE MAKEUP

5. Honor upheld

For the third and final time, The Rock and Austin fought in a main event match at *WrestleMania XIX*. Unlike their first two clashes, this contest wasn't for the WWE Championship, but The Rock wanted to prove he could beat Austin. Their back-and-forth contest ended when The Rock used his Rock Bottom move three times to pin Austin. At the end of what would be Austin's last match in WWE, the duo embraced in a show of mutual respect.

> **"You're scared, ain't ya, Rock? You're scared."**
>
> *RAW*, March 10, 2003

BRIAN PILLMAN
VS.
GOLDUST

Intensely personal, the rivalry between Goldust and Brian Pillman went back years. They were once friends, but the fact Pillman had once dated Goldust's wife Marlena came between them. By the time they were in WWE, their friendship fell apart and Pillman used their past relationship to needle Goldust until he reached his breaking point. Goldust attacked Pillman repeatedly, desperate to defend his wife's honor.

1. Going for Gold
RAW, July 7, 1997: Pillman was trained in in-ring competition by the Hart Family, in Calgary, Alberta, Canada. As such, the Hart family considered him to be a member of the family and invited him to join their Hart Foundation faction. The Hart Foundation set their sights on WWE's best. Pillman's target was Goldust, with whom he had a long personal relationship.

2. Friend to foe
In Your House: Canadian Stampede, July 6, 1997: The Hart Foundation engaged in a Five-on-Five Match in their hometown of Calgary. Pillman, as a member of The Hart Foundation, was on one side, while Goldust was on the other. The two battled each other only briefly, but it was the beginning of the end of their friendship. The Hart Foundation emerged victorious.

3. A dressing down

SummerSlam, August 3, 1997: Pillman earned the wrath of Goldust when he claimed that he was actually the father of Goldust and Marlena's daughter. Goldust challenged Pillman to a match at *SummerSlam*, where, if Goldust won, Pillman would have to compete in a dress for the next 30 days. Goldust won, after Marlena hit Pillman with a heavy purse.

"You're crazy, Pillman!"

RAW, August 18, 1997

4. Marlena's misery

In Your House: Ground Zero, **September 7, 1997:** Pillman raised the stakes to unprecedented personal levels when he challenged Goldust to another match. The stipulation for this match was that if Goldust won, Pillman would retire from WWE. If Pillman won, however, he would have Marlena as his personal assistant for 30 days. Pillman won after stealing Marlena's loaded purse and using it against Goldust.

DID YOU KNOW?

Prior to joining WWE, Pillman and Goldust (under the name Dustin Rhodes) were occasional tag team partners in WCW.

5. Tragedy strikes

October 5, 1997: Pillman treated Marlena badly during the 30 days he was with her. He made videos of himself in romantic situations with her to torment Goldust. Pillman and Goldust were set to face off one more time at the end of the 30 days at WWE's *Bad Blood* pay-per-view, but tragically Brian Pillman died in his sleep from a heart condition the night before the event.

D-GENERATION X
VS.
THE NATION

Faction warfare was common in the more risqué Attitude Era of WWE. Superstars joined with friends and allies to find greater strength in numbers. There were perhaps no other stronger factions in this period than D-Generation X (Triple H, X-Pac, Chyna, and New Age Outlaws), and The Nation, led by The Rock (including Mark Henry, D-Lo Brown, Kama, and Owen Hart). The two factions battled for dominance in the summer of 1998.

THE BREAKUP

> "Nation, it's real simple. We got two words for ya ..."
>
> —Triple H, *RAW*, July 6, 1998

1. The (in)sincerest form of flattery

D-Generation X and The Nation were each powerful factions in their own right. So they were destined to collide, and when they did, the WWE Universe knew it would be epic. DX fired the first shot by putting on a skit where they impersonated The Nation on a June episode of *RAW*. The Nation was so insulted, they battled with DX and a violent rivalry was born.

2. A shambles

RAW, June 1, 1998: The first formal battle between the two factions was a Six-Man Elimination Match with Triple H and the New Age Outlaws representing DX against The Rock, Owen Hart, and D-Lo Brown on behalf of The Nation. The Nation won by disqualification when Ken Shamrock, who also had a rivalry with Owen Hart, attacked him. Wanting to settle the issues between them, members of both teams fought back against Shamrock as the match devolved into mass chaos.

RAW, July 20, 1998: Nation member D-Lo Brown faced DX's leader and the WWE European Champion, Triple H, for the Title. While the referee was distracted by Chyna and Mark Henry battling outside the ring, The Rock attacked Triple H from behind. D-Lo capitalized on Triple H laying flat on the mat and pinned him to win the European Championship.

4. No contest

RAW, August 17, 1998: The two factions entered a battle zone on *RAW* when every member of both teams competed in a Street Fight Match. With assistance from other DX rivals, Jeff Jarrett and Southern Justice, The Rock led a multi-man assault on Triple H. There was no victor in this match, as the chaos resulted in a no-contest draw.

> **"The Rock and the World's Strongest Man, Mark Henry, are going to lay the smackdown on you!"**
>
> —The Rock (*RAW*, September 5, 1998)

THE MAKEUP

5. A new era

As summer turned to fall, The Nation disbanded, with each of its members pursuing independent singles careers. The Rock, however, continued to have issues with DX, particularly Triple H, and would for many years to come. D-Lo Brown also fought X-Pac repeatedly over the European Title. DX continued to grow in influence and added new members to their ranks, even as The Nation folded.

RIVAL FACTS

● Collectively, the members of DX won 22 championships while they were members of the faction, including WWE Championship, Intercontinental, European, and Tag Team.

● The Nation's collective trophy case includes three Championships won while part of the faction, including two reigns as European Champion and one Intercontinental Championship.

SHAWN MICHAELS

VS.

STONE COLD STEVE AUSTIN

Two of the biggest names in WWE in their generations—Shawn Michaels, the brash upstart who led the New Generation of Superstars in the early 1990s, and Stone Cold Steve Austin, who kicked down every door in front of him and became an icon during WWE's Attitude Era. Their paths crossed as they battled for a common goal: the WWE Championship.

1. Rising to captain

King of the Ring, June 8, 1997: In a taste of what was to come in the months ahead, Stone Cold Steve Austin and Shawn Michaels faced each other in a one-on-one match at the *King of the Ring* pay-per-view. The winner of the match would be named captain of a five-Superstar team that would face The Hart Foundation a month later. Austin and Michaels' competitiveness got the better of them, and they both attacked referees, leading to a double-disqualification draw.

2. Tyson in the ring

RAW, January 19, 1998: Austin won the Royal Rumble Match, therefore earning him a match at *WrestleMania XIV* against WWE Champion Michaels. Meanwhile, WWE Chairman Mr. McMahon had a major announcement to make: boxing champion Mike Tyson would be a special referee in Austin's match at *WrestleMania*. Austin took exception to that and insulted Tyson, leading to a brawl between the two.

3. A compromised referee?

RAW, **March 2, 1998:** Mike Tyson returned to *Monday Night RAW* to talk about his role as a special enforcer referee at *WrestleMania XIV*. Before Tyson could talk too much, WWE Champion Michaels confronted him in the ring. The two stood literally nose to nose, seemingly preparing for a fight. Michaels put his hands on Tyson's shirt, ripping it off to reveal Tyson was wearing a D-Generation X t-shirt! Tyson had joined Michaels' rebellious faction. What would this mean for Austin if the referee was on Michaels' side?

4. It's a knockout!

WrestleMania XIV, **March 29, 1998:** Finally the big match arrived, and Austin got his chance to get his hands on Michaels. Both Superstars gave their all in an exhausting slugfest. After the first referee was knocked out, Austin hit Michaels with his Stunner move and pinned him. Special referee Mike Tyson jumped into the ring and made a fast three count, awarding the match and the Championship to Austin! When Michaels complained to his supposed DX teammate Tyson, Tyson punched Michaels, knocking him out.

> **"Shawn, your ass belongs to Stone Cold Steve Austin."**
>
> *RAW,* February 2, 1998

DID YOU KNOW?
Prior to falling out, Austin and Michaels joined forces and won the WWE Tag Team Championship on May 26, 1997.

5. A new era

Following their *WrestleMainia* bout, Michaels retired from in-ring competition, having passed the torch of the Championship to Austin. Austin became the leader of a new era in WWE—one filled with a new attitude.

KANE VS. UNDERTAKER

These battling brothers have clashed in WWE numerous times over two decades. Bad blood boiled up between them as children, later spilling over to WWE, and igniting in some terrifying matches. At times they have briefly been allies, but before long the animosity between them flares up again, and their far-from-fraternal feelings resurface. Their warring will likely never end.

THE BREAKUP

> **"My brother the Undertaker and I bring out the best in each other and the worst!"**
> *The Twisted Life of Kane*, 2008

1. Brotherly hate
Undertaker and Kane grew up together as half-brothers, living in their family funeral home. One day, Undertaker accidentally set the mortuary on fire. For more than 25 years, he believed Kane had died in the fire—until Paul Bearer brought him to WWE. Undertaker swore he would never fight his brother, but Kane thought very differently, forcing Undertaker into matches.

2. Casket case
***WrestleMania XIV*, March 29, 1998:** At the *Royal Rumble* two months earlier, Kane had locked Undertaker in a casket and set it ablaze. After resisting fighting his brother for months, this was the final straw, and Undertaker battled his brother for the first time at *WrestleMania XIV*. Undertaker got his revenge and won the match, but Kane would face his brother again.

3. Taking a Kaning

Monday Night RAW, **June 1, 1998:** Undertaker wanted to battle Stone Cold Steve Austin for the WWE Championship at the *King of the Ring* pay-per-view, but to do that he had to defeat Kane in a Number One Contenders Match on *RAW*. After accidentally knocking down the referee and suffering interference from Mankind, Undertaker failed in his goal and lost to Kane.

4. Buried but not dead

WrestleMania XX, **March 14, 2004:** Six months earlier, Kane had interfered in a Buried Alive Match, helping Mr. McMahon bury Undertaker. Everyone believed Undertaker was gone for good, but soon Kane began to receive haunting messages from his brother, seemingly from beyond the grave. At *WrestleMania XX*, Undertaker made a shocking return, appearing alongside Kane's father and former manager Paul Bearer and soundly defeating Kane.

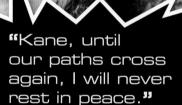

> **"Kane, until our paths cross again, I will never rest in peace."**
>
> *Royal Rumble*, January 18, 1998

THE MAKEUP

5. Band of brothers

Eventually, the dark duo learned to respect each other, even joining forces as a tag team known as "The Brothers of Destruction." They won the WWE Tag Team Championship on two occasions, and have banded together to face such powerful teams as The Wyatt Family. How long their truce will last remains to be seen.

RIVAL FACTS

- Kane has more victories over Undertaker in televised matches, although the majority have ended in no-contest draws.

- Undertaker is a seven-time WWE World Heavyweight Champion; Kane has held the Title twice.

- Kane has won a Money in the Bank Ladder Match, while Undertaker has never competed in one at all.

- Undertaker won the Royal Rumble Match in 2007; Kane has never won that match.

MANKIND

VS.

THE ROCK

There were possibly no two Superstars more opposed than The Rock and Mankind. The Rock wore expensive clothes, while Mankind had a disheveled appearance. The Rock's in-ring offense was well-practiced, while Mankind was reckless. However, they each shared one goal: the WWE Championship. This ambition brought them into direct competition with each other and created some of the most entertaining matches in WWE history.

THE BREAKUP

1. Deadly games

The Rock and Mankind's first collision occurred at the 1998 *Survivor Series* pay-per-view in the finals of the Deadly Games WWE Championship tournament. The Rock had Mankind in a Sharpshooter hold when Mr. McMahon raced to ringside and ordered the referee to ring the bell early. The Rock won the WWE Championship and joined Mr. McMahon's Corporation faction. Furious, Mankind sought his revenge.

2. First win

RAW, **January 4, 1999:** The Rock and Mr. McMahon's Corporation faction were determined to keep the WWE Championship away from Mankind. Even when Mankind earned a championship match on *RAW,* the Corporation made member Shane McMahon the special referee. The plan backfired as the rival D-Generation X faction protected Mankind from the Corporation's attack, and with added help from Stone Cold Steve Austin, Mankind pinned The Rock to win his first WWE Championship.

3. I quit!

Royal Rumble, January 24, 1999:
Less than three weeks after winning the WWE Championship from The Rock, Mankind defended it against him in an "I Quit" Match, where the only way to win is to make your opponent say the words "I quit." In one of the most ferocious matches ever in WWE, The Rock repeatedly beat down Mankind, who refused to quit. The WWE Universe was shocked when they heard Mankind's submission, giving The Rock the win. It was soon revealed that The Rock had cheated by playing a recording of Mankind saying "I quit."

> "Mankind, you realize The Rock is the Most Electrifying Man in sports entertainment today?"
>
> *RAW,* February 9, 1999

4. Empty arena

Halftime Heat, January 31, 1999:
One week after the brutal I Quit Match, Mankind got a rematch. Broadcast as part of a special edition of *WWE Sunday Night Heat* that aired during halftime of *Super Bowl XXXIII*, the rematch occurred in an empty arena. The Rock and Mankind battled all over the arena—in the audience seats, backstage, even the arena's kitchen. Ultimately, Mankind used a forklift and pallet to pin The Rock and recapture the WWE Championship.

RIVAL FACTS

● The Rock has held the WWE Championship 10 times, while Mankind has won it three times.

● Mankind is an eight-time Tag Team Champion; The Rock has been Tag Team Champion five times.

● The Rock won the 2000 Royal Rumble Match; Mankind has never won a Royal Rumble Match.

THE MAKEUP

5. Rock 'n' Sock connect

Mankind lost the Championship back to The Rock a month later and the two did r face each other again for the Title. Howe in the months that followed, they set thei differences aside and found that if they worked together, they could make a powerful team. Thus, the Rock 'n' Sock Connection was formed.

CHRIS JERICHO'S RIVALRIES

Brash. Arrogant. Obnoxious. Chris Jericho knew how to push the buttons of his fellow Superstars and the WWE Universe. Utterly convinced of his own superiority, "Y2J" refused to hold his tongue. The legendary likes of The Rock, Triple H, Kurt Angle, Shawn Michaels, and Rey Mysterio wanted nothing more than to shut him up. This wasn't easy, however, as Jericho had the in-ring skills to back up his trash-talk.

The Rock

Jericho made his debut during an episode of *RAW* on August 9, 1999, interrupting The Rock. He and The Rock traded insults, with The Rock getting the better of the newcomer. The humiliation caused Jericho to seek revenge on The Rock on several occasions over the following two years. The most significant match was for the WCW Championship at *Vengeance* on December 9, 2001. Jericho beat The Rock and won the Title. Minutes later, he would also defeat Stone Cold Steve Austin to become the WWE Champion. Nearly 20 years later, Jericho still brags about beating The Rock and Steve Austin in the same night.

Triple H

When Chris Jericho insulted Stephanie McMahon, he sparked a heated rivalry with Stephanie's husband, Triple H. Over the course of two years "Y2J" and Triple H played out their animosity inside and outside of the ring.

Their final showdown, for the Undisputed WWE Championship took place at *WrestleMania X8* in 2002. By this time, Stephanie had separated from Triple H, and, in a twist that shocked the WWE Universe to the core, she sided with Jericho, the defending Champion. This act of duplicity just seemed to inspire Triple H, who eventually gave Stephanie his trademark Pedigree finisher and then used the same move on Jericho to gain the vital pinfall and win the Title.

Kurt Angle

In the course of just one year—2000—the well-matched pair of Jericho and Kurt Angle traded numerous titles. Their matches were epics of in-ring technique as each man battled for dominance. At *No Way Out*, Angle gained the upper hand by defeating Jericho for the Intercontinental Championship. Two months later, Jericho won Angle's European Championship. At the end of the year, in their final match against each other, Angle successfully defended his WWE Championship against Jericho.

In 2017, nearly two decades after their rivalry ended, Angle—now *RAW* General Manager—congratulated Jericho on winning the United States Championship, and wished his old rival well.

Shawn Michaels

Jericho said that Shawn Michaels' in-ring performances had inspired him to become a WWE Superstar. By 2003, however, Jericho felt he'd surpassed his hero, boasting that he was better than Michaels in every way. Yet, it was Michaels who won their first match at *WrestleMania XIX*. For five years, Jericho's anger over this loss festered. Then, on the June 9, 2008 edition of *RAW*, Jericho smashed Michaels' face into a TV screen during the Highlight Reel segment.

A month later, Jericho knocked Michaels out in a match at *The Great American Bash*. Michaels sought revenge and battled Jericho in two more matches. Michaels beat Jericho in a No Holds Barred Match at *Unforgiven*, but Jericho had the last laugh by beating Michaels in their final fight—a Ladder Match for the World Heavyweight Championship at *No Mercy 2008*.

Rey Mysterio

Jericho and Intercontinental Champion Rey Mysterio were two of four Superstars competing to become the number one contender to the World Heavyweight Championship on the May 1, 2009, episode of *SmackDown*. When Mysterio eliminated Jericho from the match, Jericho attacked him and a rivalry was born.

The two battled in a series of matches in the following months, including: a singles match won by Mysterio at *Judgment Day*; a No Holds Barred match at *Extreme Rules* where Jericho beat Mysterio to win the Intercontinental Championship; and a Mask vs. Title Match at *The Bash* pay-per-view in 2009, in which Mysterio won the Championship back by hitting Jericho with a typically acrobatic springboard splash to get the vital pin.

DID YOU KNOW?

Chris Jericho used to intentionally mispronounce his opponents' names. For example, Kurt Angle became Kirk Angel and "The Heartbreak Kid" Shawn Michaels became "The Has-Been Kid."

MR. MCMAHON

VS.

STONE COLD STEVE AUSTIN

"You'll be forced to do it my way, anyway. That's the hard way."
RAW, March 30, 1998

No WWE Superstar has ever clashed with authority as much as Stone Cold Steve Austin. He was a blue collar, noncorporate "Rattlesnake" who was determined to do things his way. Austin's boss, WWE Chairman Mr. McMahon, was his opposite in every way—wealthy, power-hungry, and an enforcer of policy and his rules. Their tumultuous, repeated clashes defined a whole period of WWE history, known as the Attitude Era.

THE BREAKUP

1. The hard way

The night after *WrestleMania XIV*, in which Austin won the WWE Championship, Mr. McMahon invited Austin into the ring so he could present him with the Title. He also wanted to invite Austin to reject his "redneck" ways and take on a more corporate persona. Austin soundly rejected this by giving McMahon a low blow and chose the "hard way" of doing business by following his own path.

2. Dude Love intervenes

RAW, **April 16, 1998:** Mr. McMahon was livid with Austin's rebellious attitude. The Chairman ordered WWE Champion Austin to face him in a match on *RAW*, but there was a catch: Austin had to have one hand tied behind his back. WWE officials tied Austin's hand, but just as Mr. McMahon was about to pounce, Mick Foley's alter-ego Dude Love interrupted the match and attacked Austin.

3. With help from The Rock

Royal Rumble, January 24, 1999: Mr. McMahon and Austin were the first entrants in the 30-Man Over the Top Rope Royal Rumble Match. Austin pummeled McMahon for the first couple of minutes, until McMahon escaped under the bottom rope and hid under the ring. An hour later, as 28 other Superstars entered the match and were eliminated, McMahon returned to the ring and, with help from The Rock, eliminated Austin to win!

RIVAL FACTS

● Mr. McMahon was WWE Champion once; Austin was Champion six times.

● Austin won the Royal Rumble Match on three occasions (1997, 1998, 2001); Mr. McMahon won once (1999).

● Mr. McMahon, as Chairman of WWE, has been in charge of *RAW* through his whole career; Austin has been *RAW* General Manager three times.

4. A plan backfires

Royal Rumble, February 14, 1999: Following the *Royal Rumble*, Austin wanted one more shot at McMahon and insisted that the match take place inside a steel cage. A debuting Big Show cut through the bottom of the ring in order to attack Austin and protect McMahon. However, Big Show threw Austin so hard against the cage that he broke through and fell to the floor, winning the match.

> **"Nobody, especially Vince McMahon, tells Stone Cold Steve Austin what to do, and that's the bottom line!"**
>
> *RAW*, March 30, 1998

STONE COLD STUNNERS

Austin and Mr. McMahon's encounters often ended with the Chairman on the wrong end of Austin's Stone Cold Stunner move ....

RAW (September 22, 1997) In the hallowed halls of Madison Square Garden, Austin gave McMahon a Stone Cold Stunner for the first time.

WrestleMania 23 (April 1, 2007) Austin was special guest referee in the Battle of the Billionaires Match between Mr. McMahon and Donald Trump. In the end, Austin gave McMahon a Stunner, and sat him in a barber chair to get his head shaved—the penalty for losing.

THE MAKEUP

5. Giving up

Mr. McMahon tried and tried for years to put an end to Austin's anti-corporate rebell but Austin was too tough. Nothing McMah tried worked, and eventually McMahon gav up. Occasionally he'd try to make amends but Austin would have none of it, first insu McMahon and then hitting the Chairman with his signature Stunner move.

CHYNA VS. JEFF JARRETT

For years, Chyna had proven that she was the most dominant female Superstar the WWE Universe had ever seen. Whether she was acting as D-Generation X's bodyguard or going after other female Superstars, Chyna always made an impact. Jeff Jarrett had also made his mark as a former Tag Team Champion. Jarrett didn't believe Chyna, or any woman, should be competing in the "man's world of WWE." Chyna was set on proving him wrong.

"Jeff, you're going to see who's wearing the pants, and who's wearing your Intercontinental Title!"

RAW, September 6, 1999

1. Smashing success

RAW, **August 23, 1999:** Jeff Jarrett had won the Intercontinental Championship the night before at *SummerSlam*. He boldly put out an open contract for a match to challenge him for his newly won Title. Jarrett's former D-Generation X teammate Billy Gunn intended to sign the contract, and asked Chyna to hold it for him. Instead, confident Chyna signed it herself, to Gunn's displeasure. Jarrett jumped into the ring and smashed his guitar on Chyna, hoping to wound her before their match took place.

2. Contract negotiations

SmackDown, **September 2, 1999:** After the controversial circumstances during which Chyna had signed the Championship Match contract, Chyna agreed to settle matters with Billy Gunn in the ring. The winner of their match would get to face Jarrett. Gunn tried to make Chyna succumb with his finishing move, the Famouser. However, Triple H, Chyna's D-Generation X teammate and friend, ran to the ring and hit Billy Gunn with a Pedigree. Triple H's assist allowed Chyna to win a shot at the Championship.

6ft
(1.83m)

"Look Chyna ... you have no business being in the ring with any man."

SmackDown,
September 9, 1999

3. Gender battles

***SmackDown*, September 9, 1999:** In the weeks leading up to their match, both Jarrett and Chyna successfully competed against members of the opposite sex. Chyna battled Hardcore Holly on *SmackDown*, while Jeff Jarrett battled the longest-reigning Women's Champion in WWE history, The Fabulous Moolah. Jarrett smashed Moolah with a guitar and placed her best friend Mae Young in his patented Figure-Four Leglock.

4. Unforgiven and unresolved

***Unforgiven*, September 26, 1999:** Chyna finally got her match for the Intercontinental Championship against Jarrett. Jarrett was accompanied by his new manager Miss Kitty while Chyna was supported by The Fabulous Moolah and Mae Young. Chaos ensued when the referee got knocked out. Jarrett's former manager Debra, who had had enough of Jarrett's sexism, raced to the ring and hit Jarrett with his own guitar. Because Jarrett had been attacked by an outside party, he was awarded the victory and Chyna was disqualified.

5. A bit of housekeeping

***No Mercy*, October 17, 1999:** Because of the events in their *Unforgiven* match, Chyna was granted another shot at Jarrett and the Intercontinental Championship. Because of Jeff Jarrett's sexist belief that women should only be in the kitchen, the match was called a Good Housekeeping Match and household items such as an ironing board were placed around the ring to be used as weapons. Chyna and Jarrett used several of these items during their battle, but Chyna won the match by giving Jarrett a blow with his own guitar, becoming the first female Intercontinental Champion.

RIVAL FACTS

● Jarrett is a six-time Intercontinental Champion and a former European and Tag Team Champion.

● Chyna is a two-time Intercontinental Champion and a one-time Women's Champion.

● Chyna was the first woman to enter a Royal Rumble Match in 1999, where Jarrett was also an entrant.

KANE
VS.
X-PAC

At one time, Kane and X-Pac were the best of friends. Both felt they had been ostracized by the WWE Universe and the other Superstars for being "different." Kane was outcast because of his size and dark personality, while X-Pac was smaller than the other Superstars and rebelled against rules. The two joined forces and even became WWE Tag Team Champions. However, betrayal and heartbreak eventually led to an extremely violent and personal rivalry.

"Just like the lion roars and the chicken clucks, X-Pac sucks!"

RAW, April 8, 2002

1. A real low blow

SmackDown, October 28, 1999: Kane and X-Pac had been a successful tag team. But jealousy began to fester. Kane wanted to be a part of D-Generation X (a.k.a. DX), the faction X-Pac was in for years. On the October 28, 1999 edition of *SmackDown,* X-Pac gave Kane a low blow in the middle of a Tag Team Match against the Dudley Boyz. Following the match, X-Pac told Kane that he would never be allowed to join DX. Kane didn't take this well.

2. Bad interference

Armageddon, December 12, 1999: After weeks of Kane suffering attacks from X-Pac and his DX allies, Kane was able to face his former partner in a Steel Cage Match. Once again DX tried helping X-Pac, this time by giving him steel chairs to use. However, their interference was countered by interference from Kane's girlfriend and manager, Tori. Kane got the victory, winning the battle, though not the war.

3. Ambush!

SmackDown, **February 24, 2000:** Kane was competing in a match with Tori looking on from ringside when the members of DX suddenly swarmed into the ring. X-Pac and Triple H tied Kane to the ropes and X-Pac told Kane that Tori no longer loved him. She was now X-Pac's girlfriend. One month later, Kane was again competing in a match when Tori appeared ringside, distracting him. Kane followed her to the entrance ramp, where X-Pac leapt out from backstage and blasted Kane with a flamethrower.

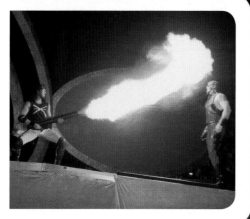

4. Kane's revenge

No Way Out Street Fight, **February 27, 2000:** In a Street Fight, there are no rules, which suited Kane just fine. He was determined to punish X-Pac and Tori as much as possible for betraying him. Kane had reunited with his father Paul Bearer and throughout the match Bearer and Kane teamed up on X-Pac. Tori watched in horror as Kane gave X-Pac his Tombstone finisher. But X-Pac recovered, and after hitting Kane with the steel ringside steps, won the match.

> **"Kane, I told you not to get involved in my business."**
>
> *SmackDown,*
> September 9, 1999

TITLE MATCHES

Kane and X-Pac's rivalry would not have been as intense if they had not been Tag Team Champions together before. They won their titles in these matches...

RAW (April 5, 1999) Kane and X-Pac won their first championship from Owen Hart and Jeff Jarrett. It appeared Kane was going to turn against X-Pac when he picked him up to slam him, but instead of slamming him to the mat, he slammed him on top of Jeff Jarrett for the pin.

RAW (August 9, 1999) The Acolytes—Bradshaw and Faarooq— had proven a formidable team, but Kane and X-Pac managed to take the Tag Team Championship from them after X-Pac hit X-Factor finishing move on Faarooq.

5. New faction same story

RAW, April 8, 2002: Kane thought his rivalry with X-Pac had ended after the Street Fight but, two years later, the rivalry was briefly renewed when Kane targeted X-Pac's new faction, the nWo. Kane challenged X-Pac to a Falls Count Anywhere Match. X-Pac lured Kane to the backstage area where his nWo teammates were lying in wait. The nWo triple-teamed Kane, beating him down with chairs, 2x4s, and more. X-Pac pinned Kane backstage and stole his mask, putting a final end to their story.

LITA VS. TRISH STRATUS

Before WWE's Women's Evolution, Lita and Trish Stratus proved that female Superstars deserved the spotlight. Trading the Women's Championship back and forth between them for the better part of a decade, Lita and Trish set the gold standard for women's in-ring competition. Athletic and charismatic, Lita and Trish inspired a generation of Superstars. Their fierce rivalry was surpassed by their well-earned mutual respect and friendship.

THE BREAKUP

1. From ringside to in-ring

Lita and Trish Stratus had both originally served as managers for tag teams in WWE, but both women wanted to compete in the ring and win the Women's Championship. These goals set them on a collision course that would change the direction of sports entertainment forever.

2. Strap match showdown

RAW, July 24, 2000: Less than a month earlier, Stratus had had her in-ring debut against Lita and The Hardy Boyz. What was supposed to be a simple tag team match, with Lita teaming with The Hardy Boyz and Stratus with Test and Albert, quickly became personal when Stratus and Lita both took their competitiveness to a more intense level. They sought to settle their differences in a Strap Match, where Superstars can use a leather strap as a weapon. Stratus won this brutal match.

Lita and Trish have faced each other in numerous "Mixed Tag Team" matches, where male and female Superstars team up. Male Superstars compete against each other and females against each other.

SmackDown (June 20, 2000) Trish Stratus, in her in-ring debut, teamed with Test and Albert (who she was managing at the time) to face Matt and Jeff Hardy and Lita. Trish and her boys were able to come out on top.

RAW (July 31, 2000) The Rock and Lita defeated Triple H and Trish Stratus when Lita pinned Trish.

RAW (June 14, 2004) Lita teamed with her longtime boyfriend Matt Hardy to successfully defeat Trish Stratus and her partner Tyson Tomko.

RAW (September 4, 2006) Less than two weeks before she would face Lita in her final match, Trish Stratus teamed up with Carlito and John Cena in a losing effort to Lita, Randy Orton, and Edge.

3. Lita takes the Championship

RAW, **December 6, 2004:** Stratus and Lita made history as the first women to compete in the main event match on *RAW*. This historic match was an incredible back-and-forth competition that showcased each Superstar's skill in the ring, but ultimately saw Lita defeat Stratus for the Women's Championship.

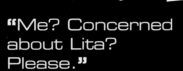

"Me? Concerned about Lita? Please."

RAW, March 14, 2005

RIVAL FACTS

● Trish Stratus is a seven-time WWE Women's Champion; Lita is a four-time WWE Women's Champion.

● Trish once won the WWE Hardcore Championship, while Lita never competed for that Title.

4. Retiring Champion

Unforgiven, **September 17, 2006:** Going into her match for the Women's Championship against Lita, Trish Stratus announced that, win or lose, this would be her final match in WWE. The contest ended when Stratus pinned Lita, winning the Championship. Emotional but victorious, Stratus immediately retired as Champion. Two months later, Lita won the Title back by winning a tournament for the Women's Championship Stratus had vacated.

THE MAKEUP

5. Famous friends

Despite their frequently vicious matches and intensity in the ring, Lita and Stratus became close friends. Their friendship, forged in the fires of mutual respect and competition, reached its pinnacle in 2014 when Stratus, who herself had entered the WWE Hall of Fame in 2013, inducted Lita into the Hall of Fame.

THE DUDLEY BOYZ

VS.

EDGE AND CHRISTIAN

VS.

THE HARDY BOYZ

Three of the greatest tag teams in WWE history emerged in 1999: The Dudley Boyz, Bubba Ray and D-Von; Edge and Christian; and The Hardy Boyz, Jeff and Matt. Brandishing steel chairs, leaping off of tall ladders, and smashing through tables, these fearless, fierce rivals were prepared to take the most extreme risks in their pursuit of coveted World Tag Team Championships— and the WWE Universe loved them for it.

2. Three-sided

WrestleMania 2000, **April 2, 2000:** The Dudley Boyz entered *WrestleMania 2000* as the Tag Team Champions, set to face The Hardy Boyz and Edge and Christian. In the first ever Triangle Ladder Match with three opposing teams, they brutalized each other until Edge threw Matt Hardy off a table that had been set up like a platform atop two ladders, and grabbed the Titles for the victory.

THE BREAKUP

1. Respect becomes rivalry

Arriving at WWE around the same time, The Hardy Boyz, The Dudley Boyz, and Edge and Christian started out with a measure of respect for each other. But as their determination to be the absolute best and win Titles gathered momentum, rivalry between these three Superstar teams grew more and more intense.

> "D-Von, get the tables!"
> —Bubba Ray, *RAW*, August 21, 2000

DID YOU KNOW?
These three teams have a combined 23 WWE Tag Team Championships between them.

3. TLC time

SummerSlam, August 27, 2000:
Tag Team Champions Edge and Christian had been attacking the Dudley Boyz with tables and the Hardy Boyz with ladders, as well as swinging chairs in a move called Con-Chair-To. The three teams battled once again, this time in the first-ever Tables, Ladders, and Chairs (TLC) Match, where Edge and Christian climbed up and retained their Championships.

4. TLC II

WrestleMania X-Seven,
April 1, 2001: As they had a year earlier, The Dudley Boyz walked into *WrestleMania* as Tag Team Champions. A second TLC Match saw Edge spearing Jeff Hardy in midair from the top of a ladder and Matt Hardy and D-Von Dudley being thrown through a stack of tables. Edge and Christian once again won the Championship.

THE MAKEUP

5. Together again

In April 2018, The Dudley Boyz were inducted into the WWE Hall of Fame by Edge and Christian. At the end of their acceptance speech, D-Von and Bubba Ray invited Edge and Christian and Matt and Jeff Hardy to join them on stage. The three teams embraced as they celebrated their historic rivalry and memorable matches. It was the first time the six Superstars had been in the same place at the same time since *WrestleMania X-Seven* in 2001.

"I can handle Christian, and I can handle Edge. I've done it before."
—Matt Hardy, *RAW,* August 3, 2000

"Hardy Boyz, we embarrassed you many times, and we'll embarrass you again."
—Edge, *SmackDown,* September 28, 2000

BOOKER T

VS.

THE ROCK

As WCW Champion, Booker T was the flag bearer for the WCW brand and proudly represented the organization. Booker T was one of the first WCW Superstars to invade WWE once Shane McMahon purchased WCW and declared war on WWE. The Rock was WWE all the way, and defended the brand with great passion and determination. The Rock was unimpressed with Booker T and made it clear every time they encountered each other.

THE BREAKUP

> **"I'm going to make an example out of you, Rock!"**
> *SmackDown*, February 7, 2002

1. The Rock's refusal

The Rock had been away from WWE while the WCW/ECW Alliance had been running through WWE Superstars. The Alliance stable tried recruiting The Rock, but The Rock rejected the invitation. Booker T, one of the Alliance's top stars, was insulted by The Rock's rejection and threatened to punish The Rock for refusing the offer. The Rock mocked Booker T, calling him a nobody, and promising to take away his WCW Championship.

2. T's last dance

SummerSlam, August 19, 2001: Booker T defended his WCW Championship against The Rock in the main event. After a bruising battle, both in and outside the ring, Booker T thought he had the match won and celebrated by breakdancing in the ring, turning his back on his seemingly exhausted foe. Suddenly The Rock leaped up and pinned Booker T with a Rock Bottom to snatch the Title.

RIVAL FACTS

- Booker T is a six-time World Heavyweight Champion and The Rock has been the top champion 10 times.

- The Rock has won the *Royal Rumble* once (2000), while Booker T has won *King of the Ring* once (2006).

- Both are former Intercontinental Champions, with The Rock holding the Title twice and Booker T once.

3. Surprise attacks

SmackDown, November 18, 2001: Booker T got a rematch against The Rock for the WCW Championship. Chris Jericho, a team member of Team WWE at the upcoming *Survivor Series* pay-per-view, attacked his teammate The Rock. Rob Van Dam, a member of Team Alliance at *Survivor Series*, attacked his teammate Booker T. These two interventions caused the match to be declared a no-contest draw.

4. Elbowed out

SmackDown, February 7, 2002: The Rock had issues with Undertaker and called him out. He was surprised when Booker T came to the ring instead. They traded verbal barbs and an impromptu match took place. The Rock used his People's Elbow move to floor Booker T and pin him for the win.

> "Just who in the blue hell are you?"
>
> *SmackDown*, August 2, 2001

TAG TEAM MEETINGS

During their rivalry, The Rock and Booker T were frequently on opposite sides of the ring in tag team matches...

SmackDown (September 20, 2001) Booker T joined forces with Test and Rhyno to face The Rock and APA in a Six-Man Elimination Match. The Rock eliminated Booker T to win.

Unforgiven (September 23, 2001) Booker T and Shane McMahon teamed up against The Rock in a Handicap Match for The Rock's WCW Championship. Neither Shane nor Booker was able to defeat The Rock.

RAW (October 29, 2001) WWE Tag Team Champions The Rock and Chris Jericho successfully defended their Championship against Booker T and Test.

Survivor Series (November 18, 2001) Team WWE (The Rock, Big Show, Undertaker, Kane, and Chris Jericho) defeated Team Alliance (Stone Cold Steve Austin, Booker T, Shane McMahon, Kurt Angle, and Rob Van Dam), resulting in the Alliance dissolving. The Rock eliminated Booker T in the match.

THE MAKEUP

5. A new respect

The Rock and Booker T went their separate ways following their match on *SmackDown*. The Rock left WWE to become a mega movie star and Booker T became a multi-time World Champion and Hall of Fame inductee. Despite their hostile history, the Superstars grew to admire one another's achievements and developed mutual respect for each other.

JEFF HARDY VS. ROB VAN DAM

Extreme means "beyond normal limits," and it could not apply to two Superstars more than it does to Jeff Hardy and Rob Van Dam, both known for their high-flying moves in the ring. Hardy was a member of Team Xtreme (with his brother Matt and their friend Lita). RVD was an icon in Extreme Championship Wrestling (ECW). When they clashed, they always took things … you guessed it … to the extreme.

1. In with a splash

***Invasion*, July 22, 2001:** Rob Van Dam came to WWE as part of the WCW/ECW Alliance faction. As a longtime stalwart in ECW, RVD had extensive experience in Hardcore Matches. At the *Invasion* pay-per-view, he challenged Jeff Hardy for the Hardcore Championship. After hitting Hardy with his Five-Star Frog Splash finishing move, RVD won the Title—his first in WWE.

2. Ladder tussle

***SummerSlam* Hardcore Ladder Match, August 19, 2001:** Hardy had recaptured the Hardcore Championship from RVD a couple weeks earlier, setting up a Ladder Match for the Title at *SummerSlam*. Hardy, a master of the Ladder Match, used the ladder to his advantage, flying from it and wielding it as a weapon. RVD took him down a rung or two when he pushed Hardy off the ladder, then climbed up to grab the Title and win the match.

3. Crashdown

***SmackDown*, August 23, 2001:** Four days after their ladder war at *SummerSlam*, Hardy was granted a rematch against RVD for the Hardcore Championship. Not far into the match, Hardy missed a dive on RVD and crashed through a table. Unable to continue, Hardy was forced to forfeit the match, which was awarded to RVD. RVD tried to help Hardy receive medical attention after his crash.

RIVAL FACTS

- Jeff Hardy is a three-time WWE World Heavyweig Champion. RVD won that Title once.

- Hardy is a three-time Hardcore Champion and Rob Van Dam a four-time Hardcore Champion.

- RVD held the Intercontinental Championship six times; Hardy held it four.

- Hardy is an eight-time Tag Team Champion; RVD is a three-time Tag Team Champion.

> **"C'mon! It's you and me, Jeff! You're next!"**
>
> *Invasion*, July 22, 2001

4. Two-in-one Title

***RAW*, July 22, 2002:** Intercontinental Champion RVD faced European Champion Hardy in a Title Unification Ladder Match. The first Superstar to climb the ladder and retrieve the Intercontinental Title would unify the two Championships and become the Intercontinental Champion. Multiple ladders were used as weapons, and both Superstars flew from atop the ladders to inflict punishment. Ultimately, it was RVD who climbed up and grabbed the Title.

5. Who's number one?

***RAW*, August 8, 2002:** Heading into *SummerSlam*, RVD and Hardy had a match to determine which of them would become the number one contender for the Intercontinental Championship. Hardy's job was made harder when his brother Matt attacked him, leaving RVD free to hit him with a Frog Splash move, win the match, and chase the Intercontinental Championship at *SummerSlam*.

SHAWN MICHAELS

VS.

TRIPLE H

It's hard to imagine any two Superstars being closer, though not actually related, than Shawn Michaels and Triple H. They were part of The Kliq, a group of five Superstars who were the very best of friends. They also co-founded the notorious D-Generation X faction together. But, like most brothers, from time-to-time, they fight. And when they do fight, it gets very, very personal.

THE BREAKUP

1. Losing the game

For four years, Shawn Michaels had been out of action due to a severe back injury. When Triple H joined *RAW* on July 22, 2002, Michaels was ordered to be Triple H's new manager. Michaels refused to be forced into anything. Triple H convinced him everything would work out, handing Shawn a DX shirt, seemingly reforming the faction. Triple H was secretly disgusted that Michaels seemed to think he was too good to be Triple H's manager and kicked Michaels, splitting up DX and their friendship.

2. Unsanctioned

SummerSlam, August 27, 2002: Triple H continued his attacks on Shawn Michaels, throwing him through a car window and beating him up whenever Michaels wasn't expecting it. Michaels, though wary of his injured back, challenged Triple H to an unsanctioned fight at *SummerSlam*. The former partners fought viciously, with Michaels getting the pin. Following the match, Triple H hit Michaels in the back with his sledgehammer.

RIVAL FACTS

- Triple H is a 14-time WWE World Champion; Shawn Michaels is a four-time WWE World Heavyweight Champion.

- Shawn Michaels was the first Grand Slam Champion in WWE (winning four different championships); Triple H was the second Superstar to become a Grand Slam Champion.

- Triple H is a five-time Intercontinental Champion; Shawn Michaels won that Title on three occasions.

- Triple H is a five-time Intercontinental Champion; Shawn Michaels won that Title on three occasions.

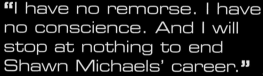

"I have no remorse. I have no conscience. And I will stop at nothing to end Shawn Michaels' career."

RAW, June 7, 2004

3. Three Stages of Hell

Armageddon, **December 15, 2002:** Shawn Michaels returned to full-time in-ring competition and won the World Heavyweight Championship at *Survivor Series*. His first Title defense was against Triple H in a Three Stages of Hell Match: the first stage was a Street Fight won by Triple H. The second was a Steel Cage Match, which Michaels won. The third fall was a Ladder Match, where Triple H regained the Championship.

4. Caged in

Bad Blood, **June 13, 2004:** Triple H and Shawn Michaels continued to battle each other for two years. They traded the World Heavyweight Championship back and forth and cost each other championship wins. In 2004, there was only one place left to settle their differences; the most intense match in WWE—Hell in a Cell. After nearly an hour of punishing each other in the steel cage, Triple H was able to rest one arm on Michaels to get a pin.

THE MAKEUP

5. DX forever

In the summer of 2006, Triple H was being targeted by WWE Chairman Mr. McMahon, who didn't like him. McMahon forced Triple H to compete against Superstars in Handicap Matches. During one of these matches against the Spirit Squad, Triple H was vastly outnumbered, but Michaels raced to the ring to save him. It was as though they'd forgotten their differences. They reformed DX and have been side-by-side, as close as brothers, ever since.

KURT ANGLE
VS.
SHANE MCMAHON

Shane McMahon, the son of WWE Chairman Vince McMahon, is a competitive guy. Almost as competitive, perhaps, as wrestling Gold Medalist Kurt Angle. Whatever either of these Superstars are striving to do, they want to be the best at it and prove their dominance over any rival. Whether competing against each other in the ring or as leaders on *RAW* and *SmackDown*, Angle and McMahon are always trying to top each other.

DID YOU KNOW?

Despite initially disliking Shane McMahon's stable, Team WCW, Angle eventually joined it and even won the WCW Championship.

1. Don't interrupt!

RAW, **May 21, 2001:** The night before the *Judgment Day* pay-per-view, Kurt Angle retrieved his stolen Olympic gold medal. He was on *RAW*, celebrating in the ring, when his party was rudely interrupted by Shane McMahon. Shane was there to announce that WCW, a rival company to WWE he had purchased a couple of months earlier, was coming back. Furious at the interruption, Angle slammed Shane.

2. Shane's Angle

RAW, **June 11, 2001:** Angle called out Shane, but was met instead by Undertaker, who accused him of stalking his wife. Angle denied it, but Undertaker attacked anyway. After a long fight, Shane swooped in to finish the job Undertaker had started. He won with an Angle Slam—Angle's own finishing move.

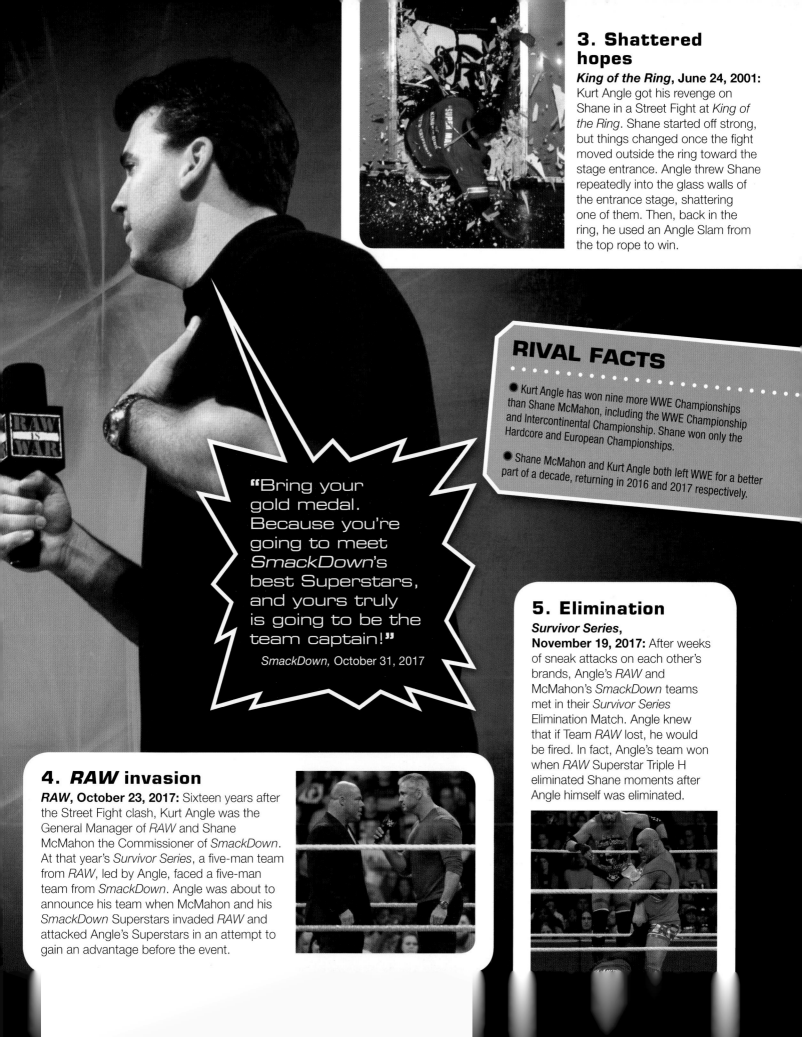

3. Shattered hopes

King of the Ring, June 24, 2001: Kurt Angle got his revenge on Shane in a Street Fight at *King of the Ring*. Shane started off strong, but things changed once the fight moved outside the ring toward the stage entrance. Angle threw Shane repeatedly into the glass walls of the entrance stage, shattering one of them. Then, back in the ring, he used an Angle Slam from the top rope to win.

RIVAL FACTS

● Kurt Angle has won nine more WWE Championships than Shane McMahon, including the WWE Championship and Intercontinental Championship. Shane won only the Hardcore and European Championships.

● Shane McMahon and Kurt Angle both left WWE for a better part of a decade, returning in 2016 and 2017 respectively.

> "Bring your gold medal. Because you're going to meet *SmackDown*'s best Superstars, and yours truly is going to be the team captain!"
>
> *SmackDown*, October 31, 2017

5. Elimination

Survivor Series, November 19, 2017: After weeks of sneak attacks on each other's brands, Angle's *RAW* and McMahon's *SmackDown* teams met in their *Survivor Series* Elimination Match. Angle knew that if Team *RAW* lost, he would be fired. In fact, Angle's team won when *RAW* Superstar Triple H eliminated Shane moments after Angle himself was eliminated.

4. *RAW* invasion

RAW, October 23, 2017: Sixteen years after the Street Fight clash, Kurt Angle was the General Manager of *RAW* and Shane McMahon the Commissioner of *SmackDown*. At that year's *Survivor Series*, a five-man team from *RAW*, led by Angle, faced a five-man team from *SmackDown*. Angle was about to announce his team when McMahon and his *SmackDown* Superstars invaded *RAW* and attacked Angle's Superstars in an attempt to gain an advantage before the event.

HULK HOGAN VS. THE ROCK

"… Someday Hulk Hogan and The Rock are going to square off one more time."

RAW, March 18, 2002

Throughout the 1980s Hulk Hogan was the biggest star in WWE. After he left WWE to create the New World Order (nWo) faction in WCW in the 1990s, Superstars like The Rock took the number one spot. When Mr. McMahon brought the nWo back to WWE to create chaos and havoc throughout the organization, The Rock saw an opportunity to confront Hogan, his childhood hero, to see who really was the better Superstar.

THE BREAKUP

1. Icon vs. icon

On Hogan's first night back on *RAW* February 18, 2002 after nearly a decade away in WCW, The Rock challenged Hogan to one more *WrestleMania* main event match to see who the biggest icon in the history of sports entertainment was. Hogan readily accepted the challenge.

2. Hogan comes out on top

RAW, **March 11, 2002:** In anticipation of the match at *WrestleMania* the following Sunday, Hogan and The Rock faced each other in a Tag Team Handicap Match. Hogan joined his nWo partners Scott Hall and Kevin Nash, while The Rock was joined by Stone Cold Steve Austin. The nWo powered through as Hogan used his Leg Drop finishing move to pin The Rock for the win.

3. A win for The Rock

***WrestleMania X8,* March 17, 2002:**
In what is considered to be one of the greatest *WrestleMania* matches of all time, Hogan and The Rock had an evenly matched contest that eventually saw The Rock defeat Hogan. Hogan, humbled by the loss, raised The Rock's hand in victory. The crowd cheered both Superstars, recognizing The Rock and Hogan as sports entertainment icons.

4. Underhanded tactics

***No Way Out,* February 23, 2003:**
Nearly a year after their epic confrontation at *WrestleMania,* Hogan and The Rock faced each other again. This time, however, while Hogan embraced the fans, The Rock turned his back on them, believing they had rejected him for choosing to pursue his movie career. Thanks to help from The Rock's allies, Mr. McMahon, and a crooked referee, The Rock defeated Hulk Hogan once again.

TAG TEAM PARTNERSHIP

Hulk Hogan and The Rock teamed up together as tag team partners on three occasions:

RAW (March 25, 2002) Hogan and The Rock battled against Hogan's now-former nWo brethren Kevin Nash, Scott Hall, and X-Pac. The match ended in a victory for the nWo when Kane interfered on behalf of Hogan and The Rock.

SmackDown (March 28, 2002) Following the events on *RAW*, Kane joined Hogan and The Rock to face the nWo. Kane pinned X-Pac for the win.

SmackDown (July 25, 2002) Hogan and The Rock competed for the WWE Tag Team Championship against the UnAmericans, Christian and Test. Hogan and The Rock won by disqualification when Brock Lesnar attacked Hogan.

> **"The Rock says ... how about headlining one more *WrestleMania* with The Rock?"**
>
> *RAW,* February 18, 2002

THE MAKEUP

5. Electrifying

The Rock and Hogan never competed in the ring against each other again, but they shared an emotional moment more than a decade later, reuniting and electrifying the fans at *WrestleMania XXX* in the Superdome in New Orleans. The Rock good-naturedly teased Hogan for misstating the name of the stadium. Together they, along with Steve Austin, toasted the WWE Universe and *WrestleMania.*

RIVAL FACTS

● Hulk Hogan is a 12-time World Heavyweight Champion. The Rock has held the Title 10 times.

● Both have been WWE Tag Team Champions—Hogan once, The Rock five times.

● The Rock is a former Intercontinental Champion. Hogan has never won that Title.

119

KANE
VS.
ROB VAN DAM

Kane is known by many nicknames including "The Big Red Monster" and "The Devil's Favorite Demon," All of these names reflect Kane's intense and fiery nature. Rob Van Dam is the opposite of Kane— always calm and collected. When the two Superstars formed a tag team, it seemed as if their unusual partnership was built on trust and mutual support. But it didn't last. Kane's internal torment spilled over and turned into violence against his unfortuante partner.

DID YOU KNOW?

Although they were tag team partners at the time, Kane eliminated Rob Van Dam from the 2003 Royal Rumble Match.

1. Unmasked and unleashed

RAW, **June 23, 2003:** Kane had hidden his face behind a mask for years, believing he was too hideous. His tag team partner, Rob Van Dam, had tried convincing him not to worry about his appearance. When Kane was required to remove his mask permanently after losing a match against World Heavyweight Champion Triple H, RVD raced to the ring to support his partner. But removing the mask caused Kane to snap. He turned his anger on RVD, chokeslamming him to the mat.

2. Screen time

RAW, **July 21, 2003:** Now unmasked, Kane focused his rage on RVD. After conducting random attacks on RVD backstage, Kane was forced to face RVD in a match on *RAW*. The two former tag team partners brawled outside of the ring, leading up the entrance ramp, before the match could officially begin. Kane hoisted RVD up, preparing to chokeslam him off the stage, but RVD escaped the slam. Kane picked him up again, this time driving him into the video screens surrounding the entryway.

3. Fire

RAW, **August 18, 2003:** RVD was competing in a match for the Intercontinental Championship against Christian when Kane came to the ring and beat RVD with a chair. The monster carried RVD backstage, where he handcuffed him to a pole and doused him in gasoline. Shockingly, Kane lit a book of matches, threatening RVD, but then he blew the matches out, saying he wasn't going to do what the demons in his head wanted him to do anymore.

4. No holds barred

SummerSlam, **August 24 , 2003:** Kane and RVD next clashed in a No Holds Barred match at *SummerSlam.* With no rules, the two combatants unleashed their most powerful moves and battled with ladders and chairs. RVD tried using one of his famed aerial maneuvers to take Kane down, but the larger Superster caught RVD in mid air, turned him upside down for a tombstone piledriver, then pinned him for the win.

> **"Kane, you should do whatever you feel is necessary to ensure your victory, dude, because you can be damn sure I'm going to make sure the winner tonight is Rob Van Dam."**
>
> *Royal Rumble,* January 19, 2003

RIVAL FACTS

- Kane and Rob Van Dam are both one-time WWE Champions.
- Both Kane and Rob Van Dam have won the Money in the Bank briefcase; RVD in 2006, Kane in 2010.
- Both Superstars have won the Hardcore, Intercontinental, Tag Team, and ECW championships.
- Kane has won the World Heavyweight Championship; RVD never won that Title.

5. Rage in the cage

RAW, **September 8, 2003:** After countless vicious encounters backstage and in the ring over the summer of 2003, RVD and Kane had their final confrontation inside a steel cage. Kane dominated the match, punishing RVD. Kane threw RVD through the cage wall, sending him to the floor outside the ring. This action technically gave RVD the win as he'd escaped the cage. But the RAW General Manager restarted the match, saying RVD didn't escape through the door or over the top of the cage. Kane once again proved his dominance by slamming RVD to the mat and pinned sealing their rivalry permanently.

MODERN
ERA

TRIPLE H VS. UNDERTAKER

Arguably the biggest Superstars in WWE during the early 2000s were Triple H and Undertaker. They both won countless championships and defeated numerous opponents. Each Superstar eager to stake out their legacy, Undertaker and Triple H's paths would collide time and time again, neither man fully demonstrating superiority over the other. Their battles would define their generation, but their differences would never be fully resolved.

DID YOU KNOW?

Triple H and Undertaker faced each other for the first time in more than six years (and 21 years after their first match against each other) in 2018 at *WWE Super Show Down*, the first WWE pay-per-view broadcast from Australia.

1. Hate at first fight

RAW, **September 29, 1997:** Triple H and Undertaker had their first ever match on *RAW*. In this encounter, the first of dozens, Triple H was helped by his D-Generation X cohorts Shawn Michaels, Chyna, and "Ravishing" Rick Rude. They attacked Undertaker and put him in a body bag, something Undertaker had been doing to his own opponents for years.

2. Forced into battle

WrestleMania X-Seven, **April 1, 2001:** Triple H believed that he deserved to be included in the WWE Championship Match at *WrestleMania*, bragging he'd beaten every WWE Superstar. Undertaker angrily reminded Triple H that he hadn't beaten him. Undertaker and Kane then took Triple H's wife Stephanie McMahon hostage, until Triple H finally agreed to a match against Undertaker. Undertaker defeated Triple H in the match, making "The Game" the ninth victim in Undertaker's *WrestleMania* undefeated streak.

3. A silent challenge

RAW, **February 21, 2011:** At *WrestleMania XXVI*, Undertaker ended the career of Triple H's best friend, Shawn Michaels, when he won a Streak vs. Career Match. When Undertaker returned to WWE after months of mysterious absence, Triple H interrupted his comeback speech and stared him down, angry about his friend's forced retirement. Silently, the two Superstars glanced up at the *WrestleMania* sign above the ring. Triple H did his DX chop gesture, Undertaker made his throat-slashing gesture, and a match was set.

"Triple H, you are standing in the middle of my yard. You don't want to be here. Bad things happen in my yard."

SmackDown, March 8, 2001

4. No rules

WrestleMania XXVII, **April 3, 2011:** Following their *RAW* stare-down, Undertaker and Triple H fought in a vicious No Holds Barred Match where there were no rules. The opponents used chairs, tables, a sledgehammer, and more to beat each other down before Undertaker finally forced Triple H to submit to his Hell's Gate submission lock. Both men later required medical attention.

5. Last of their kind

WrestleMania XXVIII, **April 1, 2012:** Undertaker challenged Triple H to a rematch at *WrestleMania*, this time in a grueling Hell in a Cell Match called the "End of an Era." Shawn Michaels inserted himself in the rivalry once again as a special referee in a match which saw the two Superstars clash for seemingly the last time. Undertaker came out on top, pinning Triple H to win. Afterward, Michaels, Triple H, and Undertaker embraced, united in the knowledge that they were the last Superstars of their generation.

RIVAL FACTS

- Triple H is a 14-time World Heavyweight Champion; Undertaker is a seven-time World Champion.

- Both Undertaker and Triple H have won the Royal Rumble Match—Undertaker in 2007, Triple H in 2002 and 2016.

- Triple H has won three Tag Team Championships. Undertaker has doubled that with six Tag Team Championship victories.

RAW VS. SMACKDOWN

First broadcast in 1993, WWE's flagship show *RAW* had seen off competition from rival companies. By 1999, WWE wanted to give its Superstars more exposure, and its growing fanbase more entertainment. The solution: A second television show, *SmackDown*. A friendly—and sometimes not-so-friendly—rivalry between *RAW* and *SmackDown* soon sprang up. Each strove to provide the most exciting show, upping the stakes every week with bigger matches featuring the most charismatic Superstars.

1. Growing the brand

When WWE purchased rival sports entertainment companies WCW and ECW in 2002, they also acquired an abundance of new Superstars for both *RAW* and *SmackDown*. Each show was given separate competitors, championships, and General Managers. WWE's then-owners, Mr. Vince McMahon and Ric Flair, each took control of one of the shows; Flair took *RAW* and Mr. McMahon *SmackDown*.

On the March 25, 2002 edition of *RAW,* Flair and McMahon drafted Superstars to their shows. From then on, pay-per-view events were split between the two brands, with only *Royal Rumble*, *WrestleMania*, *SummerSlam*, and *Survivor Series* featuring Superstars from both shows. Competition soon grew, with each General Manager striving to bring fans the greatest Superstars and the best show each week. There were trades of talent between the two shows and, every spring, the WWE Draft overhauled and refreshed *RAW* and *SmackDown*'s entire rosters.

2. Red vs. blue

A friendly battle for ratings became in-ring action in 2002, when the *King of the Ring* pay-per-view featured matches between *RAW* ("Red Brand") and *SmackDown* ("Blue Brand") Superstars. By 2005's *Survivor Series*, full teams represented their brand. At the November 27, 2005 event, Team *SmackDown* (Batista, Lashley, JBL, Orton, and Mysterio) defeated Team *RAW* (Michaels, Kane, Big Show, Carlito, and Master).

October 25, 2009's *Bragging Rights* was the first pay-per-view made up entirely of *RAW* vs. *SmackDown* matches. *SmackDown* took home the inaugural "Bragging Rights Trophy" and repeated its victory in 2010. After reaching its thrilling peak, WWE's first "brand extension" phase ended with the August 29, 2011 edition of *RAW,* when the brands were dissolved and Superstars appeared on both shows again.

3. Shaking things up

Six years later, WWE once again divided its topflight talent between the two shows. This time, the children of WWE Chairman Mr. McMahon, Stephanie and Shane, were each given control of one of the shows. On the July 18, 2016 episode of *RAW*, Shane and Stephanie hired new General Managers, with Stephanie choosing Mick Foley to lead *RAW* and Shane picking Daniel Bryan for *SmackDown*. As before, Superstars were drafted for each show, and the split between brands reinstated.

The McMahons' sibling rivalry made clashes between the two brands inevitable and increasingly personal. At 2016's *Survivor Series*, *RAW*'s men's and women's five-Superstar tag teams defeated *SmackDown*'s teams and declared *RAW* the superior show. The following year, *SmackDown* Superstars invaded *RAW* and attacked their entire roster; however, they were once again unable to defeat *RAW*'s teams at *Survivor Series*. This fierce rivalry has continued to 2018's *Survivor Series* and beyond and shows no signs of stopping.

RIVAL FACTS

● As of January 2018, *RAW* had won 24 inter-promotional singles and tag team matches while *SmackDown* had won 22.

● From July 2002 to February 2003, *SmackDown* defeated *RAW* in the ratings.

● In the 2002 brand split, the WWE Championship was *SmackDown*'s top Title. *RAW*'s was the World Heavyweight Championship. Currently, the WWE Championship is again *SmackDown*'s most coveted Title, and the WWE Universal Championship is *RAW*'s.

BROCK LESNAR'S RIVALRIES

Brock Lesnar has been a virtually unstoppable in WWE. When he debuted in 2002, he was called "The Next Big Thing," and he proceeded to prove his dominance by defeating all opposition and winning the WWE Championship just five months later. When Lesnar returned to WWE in 2012, after an eight-year absence (during which he became UFC champion), he showed that while he faced different opponents, not much else had changed. He became WWE Champion once again, and set a record as the longest-reigning WWE Universal Champion. Lesnar was still a force that few, if any, Superstars could handle.

John Cena

Lesnar and Cena's rivalry started in 2003 when Cena accused Lesnar of trying to end his career by slamming him into a ringpost. The two had a brutal match for the WWE Championship at *Backlash* (April 27, 2003), which Lesnar won. However, their rivalry did not kick into high gear until Lesnar's 2012 return to WWE when Lesnar made attacking Cena his first priority. They battled at *Extreme Rules* on April 29, 2012, with Cena just barely squeaking out a win against the dominant Lesnar.

Nearly two and a half years later, they met again, this time for the WWE Championship at *SummerSlam* in 2014. Lesnar destroyed Cena, giving him 16 of his patented German Suplexes, coining the term "Suplex City" in the process. Cena was helpless, and was never able to defeat Lesnar again.

Triple H

When Lesnar returned to WWE in 2012, he had a list of contract demands, including a private jet and renaming *RAW* after him. WWE Chief Operations Officer Triple H felt they were unreasonable. Enraged, Lesnar attacked Triple H on the April 30, 2012, edition of *RAW*, breaking his arm. Triple H challenged Lesnar to a match at *SummerSlam*, in which Lesnar once again broke Triple H's arm. Triple H returned from the injury at the February 28, 2013 episode of *RAW*, where he stopped Lesnar from injuring his father-in-law, Mr. McMahon. Triple H then challenged Lesnar to a No Holds Barred Match at *WrestleMania 29*, which Triple H won. They met a final time at May 19, 2013's *Extreme Rules*. Lesnar won the Cage Match, putting his rivalry with Triple H behind him.

Goldberg

There are some athletes who can't seem to overcome one opponent. For Lesnar, that opponent was Goldberg. The two first fought at *WrestleMania XX*. Goldberg defeated Lesnar in what was each Superstar's final match in WWE for several years. They had their first rematch at *Survivor Series* on November 20, 2016, and Goldberg defeated Lesnar in under two minutes. Humiliated by this quick defeat, Lesnar challenged Goldberg, who was the WWE Universal Champion, to a final match at *WrestleMania 33*. At that event, Lesnar shook off his Goldberg demons and defeated him for the Universal Championship.

Kurt Angle

Lesnar and Kurt Angle were both extremely talented amateur wrestlers. Lesnar had won the NCAA Collegiate Wrestling National Championship in 2000, while Angle had won the wrestling gold medal at the 1996 Olympics. When they faced each other in a WWE ring, both used all of their technical mat skills to create amazing matches.

Lesnar and Angle traded the WWE Championship back and forth over several months. Lesnar first won it by beating Angle at 2003's *WrestleMania XIX*. Angle regained the Title by beating Lesnar at the July 27, 2003 pay-per-view *Vengeance*. Although Angle successfully retained the Championship by beating Lesnar at the following month's *SummerSlam*, Lesnar defeated Angle once and for all and regained the Championship in an Iron Man Match on the September 18, 2003 episode of *SmackDown*.

The Rock

In the summer of 2002, Lesnar was a rising star in WWE. Lesnar entered the 2002 *King of the Ring* tournament, and defeated Bubba Ray Dudley, Booker T, Test, and Rob Van Dam to be crowned King of WWE. By virtue of this victory, he also was guaranteed a match against the WWE Champion at August 25's *SummerSlam*.

Another star, The Rock, won the Championship one month after Lesnar won *King of the Ring*, and Rock vs. Brock was set for *SummerSlam*. In the weeks leading up to *SummerSlam*, Lesnar interfered in The Rock's matches and mocked him in interviews. Finally, at *SummerSlam*, Lesnar easily defeated The Rock to become the new WWE Champion.

RIVAL FACTS

● Brock Lesnar, John Cena, Triple H, Goldberg, Kurt Angle, and The Rock are all multi-time WWE World Heavyweight Champions with a combined 53 reigns between them.

● Lesnar's advocate and manager, Paul Heyman, inducted Goldberg into the WWE Hall of Fame in 2018 so Goldberg could pay tribute to his greatest opponent, Lesnar.

● Lesnar caused Goldberg's elimination from the

SHAWN MICHAELS
VS.
UNDERTAKER

Shawn Michaels and Undertaker competed through the early '90s in the the New Generation, the Attitude Era, and the Modern Era. At every step of the way, the WWE legends were polar opposites. Michaels was a fun-loving symbol of hope who represented the light. Undertaker stood for darkness, despair, and evil. Whenever they met, the question was the same: Would Michaels outshine Undertaker ... or would "The Deadman" cast his grim shadow over Michaels?

> "Undertaker, make no mistake about it. I'm gonna kick your teeth down your throat ...."
>
> *RAW*, March 8, 2010

1. Michaels battles on

In Your House: Ground Zero, **September 7, 1997:** Previously, Shawn Michaels had accidentally hit Undertaker with a chair, costing him the WWE Championship. He continued to goad Undertaker with more chair attacks. Undertaker wanted revenge. When Michaels came at him with brass knuckles, Undertaker stole them and used them against him. But Michaels was not to be stopped. Eventually, the match was declared a no-contest draw.

2. Welcome to Hell

In Your House: Badd Blood, **October 5, 1997:** The rivalry between Undertaker and Michaels became so intense that WWE officials created a new match especially for them. In Hell in a Cell, opponents had to fight inside an oversized steel cage. It looked like Undertaker was about to triumph—until his brother Kane attacked him in an astonishing debut. Michaels climbed atop the fallen "Deadman" for the win.

3. King of the casket

Royal Rumble, January 18, 1998: WWE Champion Michaels and Undertaker competed in a casket match where the victor wins by putting their opponent in a coffin. Undertaker dominated the match until Michaels' D-Generation X teammates Chyna and Triple H, New Age Outlaws, tag team Los Boriquas, and even Kane all came to Michaels' aid. Undertaker was rolled into the casket, and Michaels took the win.

> **"Shawn Michaels, you will have to look me in the eye and pay for your crimes. You will rest in peace."**
>
> *RAW*, August 4, 1997

4. Back for more

WrestleMania XXV, April 5, 2009: Michaels had injured his back in the casket match and was out of action for four years. Seven years after his comeback, he challenged Undertaker to a match at *WrestleMania*. In an epic contest that saw both Superstars use their full arsenal, Undertaker won by catching a back-flipping Michaels and driving him to the mat for the pin.

5. Light extinguished

WrestleMania XXVI, March 28, 2010: Michaels was haunted by his loss to Undertaker at the previous *WrestleMania*. He demanded a rematch, but Undertaker refused... until Michaels agreed to put his career on the line. Undertaker beat Michaels, warning him to stay down; then, after executing his third Tombstone Piledriver, pinned Michaels for the win. Michaels' career in the ring was over. The light was out.

RANDY ORTON

VS.

TRIPLE H

Triple H has studied the history of sports entertainment and aimed to shape its future in his image. As such, he sought out bright young talent he could mold in his image. His greatest protégé was Randy Orton. A third-generation WWE Superstar, Orton possessed the genes of greatness—they just needed to be honed. But once Orton started fulfilling his potential, Triple H felt threatened, and chose to take down his student.

> **"The three most dominant letters on *RAW* aren't H-H-H, they're R-K-O."**
>
> *RAW,* September 6, 2004

1. D-Evolution time!

Unforgiven, **September 12, 2004:** Randy Orton had been handpicked by Triple H to join his Evolution faction so that Triple H could mentor him. When Orton won the World Heavyweight Championship, Triple H kicked him out of the group and challenged him for the Title. In that match, Triple H's Evolution teammates Ric Flair and Batista attacked Orton, helping Triple H secure the victory and win the Championship.

2. Knockout win

No Mercy, **October 7, 2007:** Triple H and Orton battled dozens of times in the three years since *Unforgiven.* At *No Mercy,* Mr. McMahon awarded the vacant WWE Championship to Orton. Triple H immediately challenged Orton for the Title and won. Later that night, Triple H had to defend the Title against Orton in a Last Man Standing Match, where the only way to win is keep your opponent down for a 10 count. Orton used his RKO move on Triple H, putting him through a table and winning the Championship.

> **"Orton, you think this is over? It's not over by a longshot. You're going to hell."**
>
> *RAW,* June 22, 2009

3. Rage in a cage

Judgment Day, **May 18, 2008:** Over the six months that followed, Triple H and Orton traded victories—and the WWE Championship—back and forth. After Triple H's Championship win over Orton in April 2008, he was forced to defend the Title inside a steel cage. Both men came close to winning by escaping the cage, but Triple H used a chair and a Pedigree to pin Orton and retain the Title.

4. For Stephanie's honor

WrestleMania XXV, **April 5, 2009:** Over another year, the rivalry between Triple H and Orton grew way more personal. Orton had won the Royal Rumble Match, granting him a WWE Championship shot at *WrestleMania XXV*. In the weeks leading up to the contest, Orton repeatedly attacked Triple H's wife Stephanie McMahon. Enraged, Triple H used a sledgehammer to punish Orton, win the match, and keep the WWE Championship.

5. Three Stages of Hell

The Bash, **June 28, 2009:** Orton and Triple H's next pay-per-view match for the WWE Championship was *Three Stages of Hell*, which included a regular match, a Falls Count Anywhere Match, and a Stretcher Match, in which the winner fastens their opponent to a stretcher. Orton won the first round after Triple H was disqualified for using a steel chair. Triple H won round two by pinning Orton. Orton's protégés, Ted DiBiase and Cody Rhodes, helped him win round three by putting Triple H on the stretcher.

BIG SHOW

VS.

JOHN CENA

In 2002, a brash rookie named John Cena made his WWE debut. He worked his way up through the best Superstars and sought to take down a veteran: none other than the "World's Largest Athlete" Big Show. Show was a multi-time World Heavyweight Champion when Cena first set him in his sights. And Show wasn't going to step aside without a fight. Their off-and-on again rivalry lasted more than a decade.

7ft (2.13m)

"Cena, I will be judging you. There will be no way out. You, my friend, I will knock out."

RAW, May 21, 2012

1. Lost opportunity
Royal Rumble, **January 25, 2004:**
Show and Cena both entered the 30-man Royal Rumble Match where the winner would get a WWE Championship Match at *WrestleMania XX*. Big Show threw John Cena over the top rope to the arena floor, eliminating him and costing him his chance at the prestigious Title. Although Show himself was soon eliminated, Cena wanted revenge.

2. A new champ
WrestleMania XX, **March 14, 2004:**
To get his revenge on his *Royal Rumble* elimination, Cena challenged Big Show to a match at *WrestleMania XX* for Big Show's United States Championship. A war of words escalated between them in the weeks prior to the match, making the bout even more personal. In the end, the relative newcomer Cena defeated veteran Big Show for the US Championship in his first *WrestleMania* appearance.

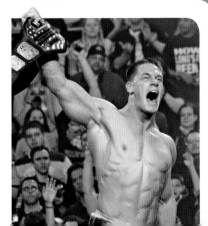

3. Thrust into the spotlight

Backlash, April 26, 2009: Following *WrestleMania XX*, the rivalry between Cena and Show was paused for a few years while each Superstar pursued other goals. But their rivalry was reignited in a match for the World Heavyweight Championship. Cena was battling in a title match with the Superstar Edge when Show appeared and attacked Cena, throwing him into a spotlight and causing a large explosion. Cena lost the match and Title. Cena sought revenge and got it a month later when he defeated Show in a match at *Judgment Day*.

"You got the franchise player on the Super Bowl stage, so let that gorilla Big Show out of his cage."

WrestleMania XX, March 14, 2004

6ft 1in (1.85m)

4. No limits

Over the Limit, May 20, 2012: Once again, a few years passed before Cena and Show renewed their adversarial relationship. *RAW* General Manager John Laurinaitis, who was due to battle with Cena, gave Show a new iron-clad contract that made him unable to be fired if he "took out" his foe John Cena. Show then attacked Cena at the *Over the Limit* pay-per-view, costing Cena his match with Laurinaitis.

RIVAL FACTS

● Cena has been WWE World Heavyweight Champion 16 times; Show has held the top prize four times.

● Show is an eight-time Tag Team Champion; Cena is a four-time Tag Team Champ.

● Both Superstars have held the United States Championship—Cena five times and Show once.

● Cena won the Royal Rumble Match on two occasions (2008, 2013) and the Money in the Bank briefcase once (2012).

5. Show down

No Way Out, June 17, 2012: After Show's attack, a cage match between Cena and Show was set with the stipulation that if Show lost, Laurinaitis would be fired. Cena hit Show with his Attitude Adjustment move and escaped the cage for the win, embarrassing Show and costing Laurinaitis his job. The loss silenced Show and put an end to his rivalry with Cena (for the time being).

EDDIE GUERRERO

VS.

REY MYSTERIO

Eddie Guerrero and Rey Mysterio's paths crossed all over the world. They had competed against each other in Mexico and Japan, as well as in Extreme Championship Wrestling (ECW) and World Championship Wrestling (WCW) before arriving in WWE. They knew each other well. Their families, who were involved in sports entertainment in Mexico (called Lucha Libre), were very close. Mysterio and Guerrero loved each other sometimes—and hated each other sometimes, too.

"Rey, I made the mistake of giving you the chance. I won't make that mistake again."
SmackDown, September 1, 2005

THE BREAKUP

1. A sore loser

Mysterio and Guerrero were so close they called each other "brother." They had formed a tag team, winning the WWE Tag Team Championship in early 2005. While still Tag Team Champs, they decided to face each other one-on-one at *WrestleMania 21,* wanting to show the world what they could do in the ring. Mysterio won the match, and Eddie did not take the defeat well.

2. Dissolution

Judgment Day, **May 22, 2005:** Mysterio and Guerrero lost their Tag Team Championship following *WrestleMania 21.* Guerrero was livid, and attacked Mysterio backstage. Keen to salvage their relationship, Mysterio challenged Guerrero at the *Judgment Day* pay-per-view, hoping to settle their issues in the ring. It didn't work: Guerrero was disqualified and, grinning, whacked the prone Mysterio with a steel chair.

RIVAL FACTS

● Guerrero was WWE Champion once; Rey Mysterio was a three-time WWE World Heavyweight Champion.

● Eddie Guerrero held the Tag Team Championship four times, including once with Rey Mysterio; Rey Mysterio was also a four-time Tag Team Champion.

● Rey Mysterio won the 2006 Royal Rumble Match, dedicating his win to Eddie Guerrero.

● Eddie Guerrero was inducted into the WWE Hall of Fame by Rey Mysterio in 2006.

3. Family first

SummerSlam, August 21, 2005:
Over the summer, Guerrero taunted and humiliated Mysterio, claiming that he, not Mysterio, was the father of Mysterio's son Dominick. Guerrero wanted custody of Dominick, but Mysterio refused. At *SummerSlam*, the two combatants had a Ladder Match where the winner had to climb a ladder and retrieve Dominick's custody papers. Mysterio and his family were overjoyed when he won the match, keeping his family intact.

4. Splash dive win

SmackDown, September 6, 2005:
Seeking another chance to hurt Mysterio, Guerrero Challenged him to a Steel Cage Match. Guerrero punished Mysterio throughout the match. He was about to exit the cage to claim the win, but changed his mind. Wishing to emphasize his dominance, he reentered the cage and leaped off the top rope in his Frog Splash dive, pinning Mysterio.

"… You've beaten your past and became WWE Champion. But you haven't beaten Rey Mysterio!"

SmackDown, July 2005

THE MAKEUP

5. A fitting tribute

Mysterio and Guerrero never competed against each other again after the cage match, as Guerrero suddenly and tragically passed away. By then, Mysterio had forgiven Guerrero, and joined with Guerrero's widow Vickie and nephew Chavo in inducting Eddie into the WWE Hall of Fame. When Mysterio won the World Heavyweight Championship at *WrestleMania 22*, he dedicated the victory and his subsequent championship reign to Guerrero.

EDGE
VS.
MATT HARDY

For many years, Matt Hardy and Lita were in a committed relationship. Deeply in love, they traveled the world as part of Team Xtreme. They helped each other win matches, and were always together. But while Hardy was injured and released by WWE, Edge fell in love with Lita and the two started dating. Hardy was heartbroken and sought revenge against his ex-girlfriend and former close friend Edge.

"My hands are shaking from real emotion... from real hate. I am more of a man than you are, Matt, in every way."

RAW, August 8, 2005

DID YOU KNOW?

Edge and Matt Hardy, along with their tag team partners Christian and Jeff Hardy were members of The Brood, a stable of Superstars mentored by vampiric Superstar Gangrel.

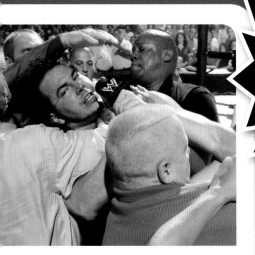

1. A man scorned

RAW, **July 11, 2005:** Lita and Edge had been married in the ring a couple weeks earlier. When the priest asked if anyone objected to the union, Edge jokingly arranged for Hardy's entrance music to blast through the arena. However, Hardy wasn't laughing and, although still not employed by WWE, began showing up at WWE events, including on *RAW*, attacking Edge backstage and during matches.

2. Grudge match

SummerSlam, **August 21, 2005:** Hardy was rehired by WWE and given a match against Edge at *SummerSlam*. There were no holds or aerial moves in this match. It was a between two men who hated each other. The match ended when Edge slammed Hardy into the ringpost. The referee called off the match because Hardy couldn't continue.

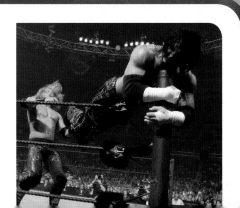

3. Street-fighting men

RAW, **August 29, 2005:** Watched by Lita, Hardy and Edge fought each other in a Street Fight a week after their *SummerSlam* brawl. Hardy leaped off a ladder, landing on Edge, then Edge smacked Hardy with a kendo stick. Hardy spiked Edge onto the steel steps, Edge replied by busting Hardy with a garbage can. The clash ended when both men fell off the entrance stage into electrical equipment, which exploded in a shower of sparks.

RIVAL FACTS

● Edge was an 11-time WWE World Heavyweight Champion. Matt Hardy never won the WWE Championship but was an ECW Champion in WWE.

● Edge is a 14-time Tag Team Champion. Matt Hardy has 10 Tag Team Championships in WWE.

4. Locked in

Unforgiven,
September 18, 2005:
After the Street Fight, there was only one more match appropriate for the venom and fire between Hardy and Edge: a Steel Cage. Despite Lita's repeated interference, Hardy climbed to the top of the cage and jumped off, crushing Edge beneath him on the mat. Hardy pinned Edge for three and won the match.

> **"Edge, I'm going to make your life miserable!"**
>
> *RAW,* July 11, 2005

SMACKDOWN RIVALRY

Years after Matt Hardy left *RAW,* Edge joined him on *SmackDown,* where their rivalry was renewed.

Non-Title Match (June 27, 2008) World Heavyweight Champion Edge defeated United States Champion Hardy (neither Title was on the line).

Brother Problems (December 19, 2008) Matt Hardy's brother Jeff had defeated Edge for the WWE Championship the night before. Still smarting from his defeat by Jeff, Edge challenged

Matt to a match and took out his resentment by beating Matt with a vicious Spear.

No Disqualification (January 16, 2009) Edge had seemingly injured Matt Hardy's brother Jeff in a pyrotechnic attack. Matt wanted revenge in the form of a No Disqualification Match. Matt was close to winning, but after interference from Mark Henry and Jack Swagger, Edge Speared Hardy for the victory.

5. Loser Leaves

RAW, **October 3, 2005:** *RAW* wasn't big enough for both Hardy and Edge. The two Superstars competed in a Loser Leaves *RAW* Ladder Match, where the winner had to climb a ladder and grab a Money in the Bank Championship contract. Hardy had the advantage, until Lita tangled him in the ropes. Edge climbed the ladder and grabbed the contact, forcing Hardy from *RAW*.

JOHN CENA
VS.
RANDY ORTON

John Cena and Randy Orton just don't like each other. Never have. Never will. They have had parallel careers, chasing the same titles at the same time—and often competing against each other for them. Their in-ring styles are similar. Both use a mix of bare-knuckle brawling and technical wizardry. Maybe it's a little professional jealousy. Maybe it's a little mutual respect. Or maybe it's just disdain. In any case, Cena and Orton are always in opposition.

> "John Cena/Randy Orton has become a rivalry. No. John Cena/Randy Orton has become THE rivalry."
>
> *RAW*, October 4, 2010

1. First fight

RAW, **November 14, 2005:** On a night when WWE was paying tribute to the late Eddie Guerrero, Cena and Orton had their first one-on-one match. Orton's father "Cowboy" Bob Orton prevented Cena from slamming Randy with an Attitude Adjustment, getting Randy disqualified. It was a hint of things to come between the two Superstars.

2. Three-way battle

WrestleMania XXIV, **March 30, 2008:** Orton had become WWE Champion. Cena, Orton's greatest rival, and Triple H, Orton's former mentor, had both earned a shot at the Title at *WrestleMania*. In the Triple Threat Match, the three Superstars fought valiantly. Triple H had Cena pinned, but Orton kicked him off Cena and pinned Cena himself for the victory, remaining Champion.

RIVAL FACTS

- Cena is a 16-time WWE World Heavyweight Champion; Orton is a 13-time WWE World Heavyweight Champion.

- Orton won the Royal Rumble Match in 2009 and 2017; Cena won in 2008 and 2013.

- Cena won the Money in the Bank Championship contract in 2012; Orton won the contract briefcase in 2013.

- Cena has been United States Champion five times, while Orton has held that Title once.

3. The unified champion

TLC: Tables, Ladders, and Chairs, **December 15, 2013:** WWE's World Heavyweight Championship, held by Cena, and Orton's WWE Championship were to be unified into the WWE World Heavyweight Championship in a TLC Match. Cena and Orton slammed each other through tables and hit each other with ladders. Orton then handcuffed Cena to the bottom rope. Cena tore the rope free to try to stop Orton climbing the ladder and seizing the Titles, but Orton hurled Cena down, knocking him out, winning the match and becoming the unified Champion.

4. Cena's day in hell

Hell in a Cell, **October 26, 2014:** Hell in a Cell is considered to be one of the most grueling, vicious matches in WWE. Orton and Cena faced each other in the cell to become number one contender for the WWE World Heavyweight Championship. When Orton hit Cena with a low blow, Cena got revenge by hitting Orton with his Attitude Adjustment move through a table for the win.

> **"John, if you get in my way, I will have no problem whatsoever putting you out of your misery."**
>
> *RAW,* October 18, 2010

5. Fighting family

SmackDown Live, **February 7, 2017:** Orton had joined Bray Wyatt's Wyatt Family stable to serve as Wyatt's protector. Cena wanted a shot at Wyatt's WWE Championship, but Orton stood in his way. With Wyatt watching from his ringside rocking chair, the two pummeled each other. Just as Cena was about to win, Wyatt attacked. However, former Wyatt Family member Luke Harper stopped the interference, allowing Cena to get the pin.

ELIMINATION CHAMBER MATCHES

Cena and Orton have competed against each other in Elimination Chamber Matches more than in any other type of match...

Elimination Chamber 2010 (February 21, 2010) Cena won the World Heavyweight Championship by beating Orton, Kofi Kingston, Ted DiBiase, Sheamus, and Triple H.

Elimination Chamber 2011 (February 20, 2011) Cena became number one contender to the WWE Championship by defeating Orton, CM Punk, John Morrison, Sheamus, and R-Truth.

Elimination Chamber 2014 (February 23, 2014) Orton successfully defended the WWE World Heavyweight Championship against John Cena, Cesaro, Christian, Daniel Bryan, and Sheamus.

BATISTA VS. TRIPLE H

Triple H and his mentor Ric Flair recognized that the future of sports entertainment relied on young Superstars developing into champion-caliber competitors. Together they recruited a pair of young lions, Randy Orton and Batista, and formed a faction called "Evolution." The name was chosen because Flair and Triple H believed Batista and Orton were the next evolution of sports entertainment. But when Batista rebelled, it brought him into Triple H's crosshairs.

THE BREAKUP

1. Thumbs down

Batista had won the 30-Superstar Royal Rumble Match, which meant he got to pick his opponent for *WrestleMania 21*—either his mentor, World Heavyweight Champion Triple H, or WWE Champion JBL. To avoid facing Batista, Triple H decided to frame JBL for an attack on Batista. However, Batista learned of the plan in advance and revealed his decision to face Triple H at *WrestleMania* with a thumbs-down gesture in Triple H's face.

2. Animal vs. Game

WrestleMania 21, April 3, 2005: Batista, who went by the nickname "The Animal," was certainly in a wild mood when he set out to battle Triple H. The match swung back and forth; both Superstars gave everything but, in the end, Batista employed his Batista Bomb move to defeat Triple H and win the World Heavyweight Championship.

4. Time for vengeance

Vengeance, June 26, 2005: Triple H was furious that he'd lost to Batista in their last two encounters. He challenged the World Heavyweight Champion to a Hell in a Cell match at *Vengeance*. The match was unbelievably brutal, with both men using a steel chair wrapped in barbed wire, a chain, and a sledgehammer on each other. By slamming Triple H on a set of steel steps, and following up with a Batista Bomb, Batista kept his Title.

3. Triple H fights dirty

Backlash, May 1, 2005: Triple H was entitled to a Championship rematch against Batista. He claimed this rematch at *Backlash*. Leading up to the event, Triple H attacked Batista backstage and in the ring. But in the match itself, although Triple H fought dirty with low blows and sneak attacks from Evolution teammate Ric Flair, he was unable to defeat Batista, who used a Batista Bomb for the win.

> "Batista isn't smart enough to know what's best for him."
>
> *RAW*, February 21, 2005

RIVAL FACTS

- Triple H is a 14-time WWE World Heavyweight Champion; Batista is a six-time champion.

- Batista won four Tag Team Championships in WWE, while Triple H won three.

- Both Superstars won the Royal Rumble Match twice—Triple H in 2002 and 2016, Batista in 2005 and 2014.

THE MAKEUP

5. No hard feelings

A few weeks after *Vengeance*, Batista was traded from *RAW* to *SmackDown*, meaning he was now a part of different WWE brand than Triple H, thus putting an end to their rivalry. Feeling he'd accomplished all he'd set out to do, Batista left WWE in 2010, only to return and reform Evolution with Triple H in December 2013.

MICKIE JAMES

VS.

TRISH STRATUS

Both Trish Stratus and Mickie James have achieved legendary status in the eyes of the WWE Universe because of their incredible in-ring ability and chemistry when competing. Throughout their time in WWE, Stratus and James raised the bar for women's competition and created countless memorable moments as James challenged Stratus and eventually earned her respect.

> **"We could've been beautiful together, Trish Stratus, but instead I'm going to beat you and take your Championship."**
>
> *RAW*, March 20, 2006

1. Fanatic
RAW, October 10, 2005: Mickie James was a huge fan of Trish Stratus. On the October 10, 2005, episode of *RAW*, she jumped from the audience to save Stratus from an attack by Superstar Victoria. In the weeks that followed, James publicly demonstrated her love for Stratus, even dressing up as Stratus for a Halloween costume contest on *RAW*.

2. The sincerest flattery
New Year's Revolution, January 8, 2006: Hoping it would bring them closer, James set out to win Stratus' WWE Women's Championship. James won a contest granting her a title shot against Stratus at *New Year's Revolution*. In the match, James used some of Stratus' own signature moves against her. Stratus countered them and pinned James to retain the Championship. However, James continued her stalking ways.

3. James ascends

***WrestleMania 22,* April 2, 2006:** Fed up with James' obsession for her, Stratus demanded to face her at *WrestleMania 22.* The two women beat each other brutally throughout the match. Eventually, James landed her signature Mick Kick move to defeat Status and win the WWE Women's Championship. Following the match, James blew Stratus a kiss.

4. Turnabout

***RAW,* April 17, 2006:** Following her win at *WrestleMania 22,* James continued to dress like Stratus. Stratus turned it around and started dressing like James. The mind games continued when James kidnapped Stratus' boyfriend. Stratus, still dressed as James, came to the rescue, attacking James and saving her boyfriend. It all led to a Championship rematch at *Backlash* two weeks later...

TAGGING AND SNAPPING

After her debut, James formed a tag team with Stratus. However, teaming up did not prevent James snapping in the run-up to their match at *WrestleMania 22.*

RAW (October 17, 2005) A team of Trish Stratus, Mickie James, and Ashley Massaro lost to Candice Michelle, Victoria, and Torrie Wilson.

RAW (November 28, 2005) Trish Stratus, Mickie James, and Ashley Massaro got revenge by defeating the three-woman team of Candice Michelle, Victoria, and Torrie Wilson

Saturday Night's Main Event (March 18, 2006) Trish Stratus and Mickie James defeated Candice Michelle and Victoria. Following the match, James attacked Stratus for not loving her enough. This would be the last time they teamed together.

5. Illegal moves

***Backlash,* April 30, 2006:** At *Backlash,* James used her wristband to illegally choke Stratus and was disqualified. Although she lost the match, James didn't lose her Championship, as titles could not change hands on a disqualification. They competed one more time for the Title in the summer of 2006, with James retaining the Title. A few months later, Stratus retired, leaving fans to wonder who was truly more dominant.

EDGE VS. JOHN CENA

John Cena's motto is "Hustle, Loyalty, Respect." That means he's always upfront about things. He confronts people face to face and he never backs down from a challenge. Edge, whose nickname is "The Rated R Superstar," is the opposite. He is sneaky, prepared to cut corners and stab people in the back to achieve his goals. Cena finds that kind of approach to life disgusting, and has tried to teach Edge a lesson in fighting like a man, instead of a shortcut-taking coward!

DID YOU KNOW?
Edge once went to John Cena's home in Boston to attack Cena's father, John Cena, Sr.

1. Cashing in

New Year's Revolution, **January 8, 2006:** Edge had won the very first Money in the Bank Ladder Match, guaranteeing him a shot at the WWE Championship whenever he wanted one. He picked *New Year's Revolution* pay-per-view, where Cena had just finished a grueling title defense inside the Elimination Chamber. Exhausted and hurting, Cena couldn't defend himself against Edge's attack. Edge won the WWE Championship in under two minutes.

2. Cheating doesn't pay

Royal Rumble, **January 29, 2006:** Three weeks after Edge's cunning Money in the Bank cash-in, Cena had a chance to win back the WWE Championship. Cena quickly went after Edge, but Edge's girlfriend, Lita, interfered, distracting Cena. Edge tried spearing Cena, but Cena dodged, resulting in Edge spearing Lita! Cena locked Edge in his STF submission hold, forcing Edge to tap out and giving Cena the Championship win.

3. An attitude adjusted

RAW, **December 25, 2006:** The rivalry between Edge and Cena went global over Christmas in 2006, when the two competed in Iraq as part of WWE's "Tribute to the Troops" episode of *RAW*. Cena was the WWE Champion, and although this was a nontitle match, Edge wanted to prove he could defeat Cena to get a Championship Match at a later time. Cena won with an Attitude Adjustment slam.

TRIPLE THREATS

Many of the battles between Cena and Edge have been in Triple Threat Matches for the WWE World Heavyweight Championship.

Backlash (April 30, 2006) John Cena retained the World Heavyweight Championship by beating Edge and Triple H.

RAW (July 3, 2006) Edge defeat Cena and Rob Van Dam to win the WWE Championship.

WrestleMania 25 (April 5, 2009) Cena became the new World Heavyweight Champion by beating Edge and Big Show.

RAW (May 24, 2010) Edge became number one contender to the World Heavyweight Championship by defeating Cena and Chris Jericho.

4. Hometown hero

RAW, **March 2, 2009:** In his hometown of Boston, Massachusetts, Cena challenged World Heavyweight Champion Edge for the Title. It looked as though Cena was about to win the match when Edge, who called himself "The Ultimate Opportunist," grabbed the Championship Title and hit Cena with it. The referee spotted the illegal hit and disqualified Edge, giving Cena the win but not the Championship.

> "The Rated R Superstar is gonna be rated G. G as in gone. As in the WWE Title is gonna be gone and to ME."
>
> *RAW*, January 23, 2006

5. The last man

***Backlash*,** **April 26, 2009:** Cena had won the World Heavyweight Championship at *WrestleMania XXV*. Edge, enraged, challenged Cena to defend the Title in a Last Man Standing Match, where the only way to win is to beat your opponent so much he can't answer a 10 count. Cena and Edge fought hard, until Big Show interfered and slammed Cena through a spotlight to win Edge the Championship.

RIVAL FACTS

- Cena won the WWE World Heavyweight Championship 16 times; Edge was an 11-time champion.

- Edge held the WWE Tag Team Championship 14 times; Cena had the Tag Team Championship four times.

- Edge was inducted into the WWE Hall of Fame in 2012; Cena has not yet been inducted.

- Edge won the very first Money in the Bank contract in 2005; Cena won it in 2012.

BATISTA VS. UNDERTAKER

> **"Our battles have taken a toll on me, but they've left me with a lot of confidence. I'm ready to go to war!"**
>
> *SmackDown*, December 7, 2007

When Undertaker and Batista battle one another, it often leaves chaos in its aftermath. Both Superstars are gigantic, powerful men who strive to be the very best in WWE. They are both focused on their objective of being WWE World Heavyweight Champion, and will destroy anything or anyone who stands in their way—especially each other.

IN THE CAGE

Undertaker and Batista took their disdain to a new level by competing in all three types of cage matches: Steel Cage, Hell in a Cell, and Elimination Chamber.

SmackDown (May 11, 2007) This Steel Cage Match ended in a draw when both Undertaker and Batista escaped the cage at the same time.

Survivor Series (November 18, 2007) Inside the mammoth Hell in a Cell cage, Batista defeated Undertaker to retain the World Heavyweight Championship.

No Way Out (February 17, 2008) Undertaker defeated Batista, Big Daddy V, Finlay, MVP, and The Great Khali in the Elimination Chamber cage.

6ft 6in (1.98m)

1. Strike one

WrestleMania 23, April 1, 2007: Undertaker won the Royal Rumble Match, earning him a *WrestleMania* match against World Heavyweight Champion Batista. After several sneak attacks by Undertaker, Batista declared he'd lost respect for him. Batista fought hard, but not hard enough. Undertaker gave him a Tombstone piledriver and pinned him to win the Title.

2. No men standing

Backlash, April 29, 2007: Four weeks after losing his title, Batista was given a rematch against Undertaker for the World Heavyweight Championship in a Last Man Standing Match. They had to battle each other until one of them couldn't answer a 10 count. Batista and Undertaker took the battle to the entrance stage, where Batista speared Undertaker off the stage to the floor. Neither man was able to stand before the 10 count, resulting in a draw.

3. Rattlesnake referee

Cyber Sunday, **October 28, 2007:** Batista had won the World Heavyweight Championship back in May 2007, injuring Undertaker in the process. When Undertaker returned he wanted payback. The resulting match occurred at *Cyber Sunday* where the WWE Universe voted on stipulations for matches. They chose Stone Cold Steve Austin as the referee for the Batista vs. Undertaker match. Batista was able to defeat Undertaker and hold on to his Championship.

6ft 10in (2.08m)

4. Weekly meetings

SmackDown, **April 18 & 25, 2008:** Six months after their brawl at *Cyber Sunday*, the pair's roles had reversed. Undertaker had won the World Heavyweight Title from Edge two weeks earlier at *WrestleMania XXIV*, meaning he was defending the Championship when he faced Batista on the April 18 edition of *SmackDown*. That match ended in a double countout draw, so they met again the following week, this time in a no countout/no disqualification match, which Undertaker won.

> "Batista, without death there can be no life. All things must die. Your reign as champion will rest in peace."
>
> *SmackDown*, March 2, 2007

RIVAL FACTS

● Undertaker is a seven-time WWE World Heavyweight Champion, while Batista was crowned Champion six times.

● Undertaker held WWE Tag Team Championships seven different times; Batista was a Tag Team Champion four times.

● Batista won the Royal Rumble Match twice (2005, 2014); Undertaker won once in 2007.

5. A bout and out

TLC: Tables, Ladders, and Chairs, **December 13, 2009:** Eighteen months after their last bout, Batista won a match earning the right to face Undertaker in a Chairs Match for his World Heavyweight Championship. Batista used a low blow to seemingly win the match, but *SmackDown* General Manager Theodore Long restarted the match, allowing Undertaker to hit Batista with a chair and win to retain the Title. Batista left WWE not long after this match, putting the rivalry to an end.

BOBBY LASHLEY
VS.
UMAGA

The word "champions" can mean more than simply the winner of a competition. It can also refer to an individual who represents another person or cause. It was the latter meaning that led to the rivalry between Bobby Lashley and Umaga. The two Superstars were selected to represent Donald Trump and Vince McMahon respectively in a match. Their rivalry grew beyond representing those billionaires and became a bitter battle for the Intercontinental and ECW Championships.

1. Battle of the billionaires

WrestleMania 23, April 1, 2007: Donald Trump and Vince McMahon had selected ECW Champion Bobby Lashley and Intercontinental Champion Umaga to represent them in a Hair vs. Hair Match. The eyes of the world were on WWE as the two Superstars defended their patrons in a brutal match. Lashley defeated Umaga, resulting in Mr. McMahon getting his head shaved by Lashley, Trump, and the match's special referee Stone Cold Steve Austin.

2. Team McMahon

Backlash, April 29, 2007: Reeling from the humiliation of the head-shaving incident, Mr. McMahon targeted Lashley for revenge. To help, he enlisted his son Shane McMahon and Umaga. Calling themselves "Team McMahon," the devious trio faced Lashley at Backlash in a three-on-one match for the ECW Championship. Umaga dove off the top rope onto Lashley before tagging in his boss. Mr. McMahon then pinned Lashley to win the match and the ECW Championship.

"Umaga will destroy you!"

—Vince McMahon,
RAW, March 12, 2007

3. A sequel

Judgment Day, May 20, 2007: Bobby Lashley demanded a rematch against Mr. McMahon for the ECW Championship. Mr. McMahon agreed as long as it was another three-on-one handicap match with Umaga and Shane McMahon by his side. Bobby Lashley fought hard against the odds, pinning Shane at the end of the match. Lashley believed he'd won back the ECW Championship, but McMahon said since Lashley didn't pin him personally, Lashley hadn't won the Title.

4. Running the gauntlet

RAW, May 21, 2007: Lashley challenged Vince McMahon to one more match for the ECW Championship. McMahon agreed if Lashley could first defeat four Superstars in succession, including Umaga and Shane McMahon. Lashley quickly tore through his first two opponents, Chris Masters and Viscera, in his four-part Gauntlet Match. Umaga used a steel chair to attack Lashley in their match, seemingly softening him up for Shane. However, Lashley overcame the odds and defeated Shane to earn his Title Match against Mr. McMahon.

DID YOU KNOW?

Umaga's cousin, Roman Reigns, has since continued the family rivalry with his own battles with Bobby Lashley.

5. To the streets

One Night Stand, June 3, 2007: Bobby Lashley finally got his shot at Mr. McMahon's ECW Championship in a Street Fight, where rules don't apply. Umaga and Shane McMahon did as much of the fighting in the match as they could. Lashley dodged a hit with a garbage can from Shane, which accidentally hit Umaga instead. This allowed Lashley to spear tackle Mr. McMahon to win the ECW Championship and finally move on from the conflict with the McMahons and Umaga.

BETH PHOENIX

VS.

MELINA

Melina came to WWE as part of the MNM stable with Joey Mercury and John Morrison. She was a Hollywood A-lister who loved everything about the lifestyles of the rich and famous. Beth Phoenix, who called herself the "Glamazon," lured Melina away from Hollywood to act as her tag team sidekick. Together Beth and Melina were a talented and terrifying duo among the female Superstars in WWE—until their alliance suddenly fractured...

"After I dispose of Melina, I'll once again be WWE Women's Champion."

RAW, May 12, 2008

1. Lumberjill match
***WrestleMania XXIV*, March 30, 2008:** With several of their WWE peers surrounding the ring in a "Lumberjill Match," Phoenix and Melina competed in a tag team match against Maria Kanellis and Ashley Massaro. Thanks to Phoenix's incredible strength, and despite interference on behalf of Maria and Ashley by Jerry Lawler, she and Melina won when Phoenix (thanks to interference from Santino) pinned Maria.

2. Tag team implosion
***RAW*, May 12, 2008:** Following their dominant performance at *WrestleMania*, Phoenix and Melina continued their success, until they met on *RAW*. They were facing Maria Kanellis and Mickie James when Melina accidentally knocked Phoenix off the ring apron. Thinking Melina had hit her on purpose, Phoenix left the match, abandoning Melina. After the match, Melina attacked Phoenix backstage, bringing an abrupt end to their friendship.

3. Winners never quit

One Night Stand, **June 1, 2008:**
After three weeks of attacking each other backstage, Phoenix and Melina went one-on-one in the first ever women's I Quit Match in WWE history. Both women used a variety of submission holds to try to make their opponent say "I quit," inflicting a lot of pain. Melina especially showed incredible flexibility to withstand Phoenix's holds, but eventually she could resist no longer and cried "I quit."

> **"She may be strong, but Beth Phoenix will not break me. She will not break me!"**
>
> *RAW*, May 19, 2008

4. Comeback win

Royal Rumble, **January 25, 2009:**
In the months that followed, Melina took some time away from WWE to rehabilitate from her injuries. While she was gone, Phoenix won the WWE Women's Championship. Upon Melina's return, she won a six-woman battle royal to become number one contender for the Women's Title. At *Royal Rumble*, Melina escaped a slam attempt by Phoenix, and surprised her with a pin to win the Championship.

5. A last goodbye

RAW, **February 16, 2009:** Less than a month after winning the Women's Championship, Melina defended it against Beth Phoenix on *RAW*. Phoenix had aligned herself with Santino Marella and Rosa Mendez, who accompanied her to ringside and attacked Melina when the referee wasn't looking. Superstars Mickie James, Kelly Kelly, and Candice Michelle ran to ringside to get rid of Santino and Rosa, allowing Melina to get the win. A few weeks later, Melina was drafted to *SmackDown* while Beth stayed on *RAW*, putting an end to their rivalry.

EDGE VS. UNDERTAKER

For nearly two decades, Undertaker had proved himself to be virtually unstoppable. Edge, on the other hand, had shown that he was a snake-in-the-grass, attacking when it served him. When Edge cashed in his Money in the Bank contract on Undertaker to win the World Heavyweight Championship, it wasn't personal. Neither were the other times Edge attacked, costing Undertaker the Title. It was about Edge wanting the gold.

> **"No one will remember the Undertaker. He will be eclipsed by one man—me!"**
>
> *SmackDown,*
> March 28, 2008

1. A hellish finish

WrestleMania XXIV, **March 30, 2008:** Undertaker had won an Elimination Chamber Match to become the number one contender for Edge's World Championship. Edge had been a thorn in Undertaker's side for the last year, and Undertaker was ready to destroy him. Catching Edge when he attempted a spear, Undertaker locked in his Hell's Gate hold to win the match and the Title.

2. No release, no relief

Backlash, **April 27, 2008:** Undertaker was forced into a rematch against Edge at the pay-per-view following *WrestleMania—Backlash*. Undertaker made quick work of Edge, defeating him to retain the Title by using a chokehold/leg lock submission hold. Undertaker refused to release it, even after winning the match. Edge had to be taken to the locker room for medical evaluation.

3. Up for grabs

Judgment Day, **May 18, 2008:** *SmackDown* General Manager (and Edge's wife) Vickie Guerrero stripped Undertaker of the World Heavyweight Championship and banned his chokehold move because he had used it to injure Edge. Undertaker and Edge competed for the vacant championship at the next pay-per-view, *Judgment Day*. Undertaker threw Edge out of the ring into the crowd, resulting in Edge being counted out. Undertaker won the match, but the Title remained vacant because it was a countout win.

> **"Edge, death waits for no man!"**
>
> *SmackDown,*
> February 29, 2008

4. Golden climb

One Night Stand: Extreme Rules, **June 1, 2008:**
Once again fighting for the vacant Championship, Edge and Undertaker entered a Tables, Ladders, and Chairs Match. If Undertaker lost, he'd be forced to leave WWE. Undertaker punished Edge repeatedly, including slamming him off a ladder through two tables. But with the help of his friends Chavo Guerrero and Bam Neeley, Edge recovered, climbed the ladder, and grabbed the Championship.

RIVAL FACTS

• Edge is an 11-time WWE World Heavyweight Champion; Undertaker has won the top prize seven times.

• Edge won the 2010 *Royal Rumble*; Undertaker won the *Royal Rumble* in 2007.

• Edge is a 14-time Tag Team Champion; Undertaker has been Tag Team Champion seven times.

• Edge has won the United States Championship, Intercontinental Championship, King of the Ring, Money in the Bank, and been inducted into the WWE Hall of Fame.

• Undertaker is a former Hardcore Champion and had a 21-match undefeated streak at *WrestleMania*.

5. Ring of fire

SummerSlam, **August 17, 2008:** Vickie Guerrero reinstated Undertaker when she learned that Edge, who had lost the World Championship to CM Punk, was cheating on her. For extra revenge on her cheating husband, she forced him into a Hell in a Cell Match with Undertaker. Undertaker used chairs, a version of Edge's Spear, and more against Edge. In the end, Undertaker chokeslammed Edge through the ring, and flames shot up from the hole in the mat; Edge had been sent straight to hell.

LAYCOOL
VS.
MICKIE JAMES

Layla and Michelle McCool were talented competitors in the ring and together made up the formidable team, LayCool. Out of the ring, however, they were nasty bullies who tried to browbeat the other female Superstars whenever they could. They gave their rivals mean nicknames and made fun of their looks, clothes, and in-ring ability. Mickie James was a strong WWE veteran and made it her mission to stop LayCool's bullying for good.

DID YOU KNOW?

LayCool were the only co-Divas Champions in WWE history, cutting the Title in half and defending it in tandem.

1. Cruel jibes

SmackDown, November 20, 2009
LayCool had been taunting and mocking Mickie James for a while, but on the November 20, 2009 edition of *SmackDown*, they took their bullying to a new level. They gave Mickie a new nickname, "Piggy James," and in the weeks that followed, they sang songs and made snorting noises at James, sometimes bringing her to tears.

2. Distracting Divas

TLC: Tables, Ladders, and Chairs, December 13, 2009: In a Divas Championship Match, Mickie James was all fired up not just to take Michelle McCool's Title but to rip McCool apart for bullying her. James started the match doing just that, but partway through Layla distracted Mickie from outside the ring. This trick gave McCool the chance to hit James with a cheap shot, pin her for the win, and retain her Championship.

3. Kick start

Royal Rumble, January 31, 2010: Because of Layla's interference in their previous match, Mickie James was granted another shot at McCool's Divas Championship at the *Royal Rumble*. Layla stood ringside taunting James. When McCool accidentally kicked Layla, Mickie used the opportunity to hit McCool with a DDT move, winning the Championship. Mickie celebrated by shoving cake into LayCool's faces!

4. Rematch clause

SmackDown, **February 26, 2010:** Whenever a WWE Champion loses their Title, they are entitled to a rematch to try to win it back. On the February 26, 2010 edition of *SmackDown*, Michelle McCool exercised her rematch clause to face Mickie James for the Divas Championship. *SmackDown* General Manager Vickie Guerrero, who had a grudge against Mickie, was the special referee. Guerrero attacked James, enabling McCool to regain the Championship.

> **"LayCool ... you're only happy at the misery of everyone else's lives when deep down inside you know you're nothing."**
>
> *SmackDown,* January 22, 2010

RIVAL FACTS

- Between them, the two members of LayCool were four-time WWE Women's and Divas Champions; Mickie James alone was a six-time Women's and Divas Champion.

- Michelle McCool and Mickie James both competed in the Inaugural Women's Royal Rumble Match in 2018.

MULTI-WOMEN TAGS

LayCool and Mickie James often got backup from other female Superstars when they faced each other. These multi-women tag team matches made for many exciting and unexpected moments.

Survivor Series (November 22, 2009) In a traditional *Survivor Series* Elimination Match, Mickie James joined with Melina, Eve Torres, Kelly Kelly, and Gail Kim to defeat Layla, Michelle McCool, Beth Phoenix, Alicia Fox, and Jillian Hall.

RAW (March 22, 2010) Mickie James and Kelly Kelly were ringside enforcers for their friends Eve Torres, Beth Phoenix, and Gail Kim as they lost to Layla, Michelle McCool, and Maryse with Vickie Guerrero and Alicia Fox as their enforcers.

WrestleMania XXVI (March 28, 2010) Michelle McCool, Layla, Mayse, Vickie Guerrero, and Alicia Fox defeated Mickie James, Beth Phoenix, Gail Kim, Kelly Kelly, and Eve Torres in a 10-woman tag team match.

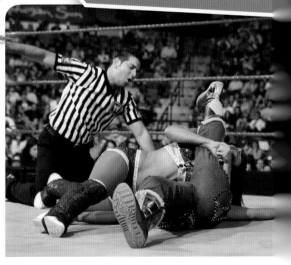

5. A little help

SmackDown, **April 23, 2010:** Mickie James never got another one-on-one match against Michelle McCool, but did get a small chance at revenge against LayCool. On the April 23, 2010 episode of *SmackDown*, James partnered with Beth Phoenix in a tag team match against LayCool. Although she fought valiantly, it was a losing effort for Mickie as Layla pinned her. It was to be Mickie James' last match in WWE for six years.

JOHN CENA VS. THE ROCK

RIVAL FACTS

● Cena is a 16-time WWE World Heavyweight Champion; The Rock has been WWE World Heavyweight Champion 10 times.

● The Rock is a five-time Tag Team Champion; Cena has won the Tag Team Championship four times.

● The Rock won the Royal Rumble Match in 2000; Cena won the Royal Rumble Match in 2008 and 2013.

Both multi-time World Champions, big names in Hollywood, passionate and driven in everything they did, the two biggest icons in modern sports entertainment were so similar in experience and success that they came to resent each other. What started as simply teasing between John Cena and The Rock gradually escalated. Soon there was only one place their rivalry could be settled: on the grandest stage of all, *WrestleMania*.

THE BREAKUP

"I am not The Rock's equal. I am better than The Rock."

RAW, April 1, 2013

1. Trading insults

After seven years away from WWE, The Rock returned, announcing he was going to be the host of *WrestleMania XXVII*. The Rock took a few minutes to soak up the love from the WWE Universe, and then declared war on John Cena. The Rock mocked Cena's dress sense, in-ring ability, and movies. Cena responded by slating The Rock for leaving WWE and only pretending to care about sports entertainment.

2. Challenge accepted

RAW, **April 4, 2011:** As guest host of *WrestleMania XXVII*, The Rock made his presence felt in the main event between Cena and WWE Champion The Miz. The Rock hit a Rock Bottom on Cena, costing him the match. The next night on *RAW*, Cena challenged The Rock to a match at the following year's *WrestleMania XXVIII*. Standing nose-to-nose with Cena, The Rock accepted.

> "John Cena, I came back to WWE to beat you."
>
> *RAW,* March 27, 2012

3. Once in a lifetime

WrestleMania XXVIII, April 1, 2012: For one year, the WWE Universe anticipated the *WrestleMania* showdown—billed as a Once in a Lifetime match—between The Rock and Cena. It seemed as if Cena was going to win, but he mistakenly took time to mock The Rock by doing his People's Elbow move. The Rock surprised Cena by leaping to his feet, slamming Cena to the mat for the pin, and stealing victory from Cena's hands.

4. Honors even

WrestleMania 29, **April 7, 2013:** The Rock had become WWE Champion, and Cena had won the Royal Rumble Match to earn a Championship Match at *WrestleMania*. So, the two titans faced each other for the last time. The outcome was very different: Cena was more focused than in their previous clash and he defeated The Rock to win the WWE Championship.

THE MAKEUP

SMACK-TALKING

The Rock and Cena reserved some of their best zingers for each other ....

RAW (February 14, 2011) "John Cena, you come out here with your bright purple shirt, before that your bright green shirt, before that your bright orange shirt. Running around here like a big fat bowl of Fruity Pebbles." —The Rock

RAW (February 21, 2011) "I wasn't talkin' trash, Rock, I was talkin' truth. You left us high and dry to play a fairy with a tooth?" —John Cena

RAW (March 5, 2012) "The Rock's best stuff has been prerecorded or by satellite." —John Cena

RAW (April 4, 2011) "You're wrong about one thing, John Cena. You're wrong about respect. You see, The Rock respects you. The Rock just doesn't like you." —The Rock

5. Making a save

The Rock returned to WWE once again at *WrestleMania 32*. He insulted Bray Wyatt and The Wyatt Family, resulting in The Wyatt Family surrounding the ring and encroaching on him. Just as the Wyatts began their four-on-one assault of The Rock, Cena, not one to stand for foul play, charged to The Rock's aid. The two embraced, solidifying a new friendship.

DANIEL BRYAN
VS.
THE MIZ

It's an understatement to say that Daniel Bryan and The Miz dislike each other. The Miz thinks that Bryan should respect him for his accomplishments in WWE and Hollywood. Bryan believes The Miz should respect him for fighting his way up from small sports entertainment companies around the world and clawing his way to the top of WWE. This mutual lack of respect has set them consistently at odds.

"Miz … you wrestle like a coward."

Talking Smack,
August 23, 2016

1. Menacing mentor

NXT, **February 23, 2010:** In its original form, WWE series *NXT* was a reality show where rookie Superstars were paired with veterans to teach them the ways of WWE. The Miz was assigned as Daniel Bryan's mentor, and the two did not get along. The Miz berated his mentee constantly, and Bryan was quickly eliminated from the competition. The Miz continued to insult Bryan, even after he was no longer his mentor.

2. The protégé strikes back

RAW, **May 31, 2010:** Bryan had had enough of the abuse leveled at him by his old mentor and was elated when *RAW* guest host and actor Ashton Kutcher granted him a match against The Miz. Bryan was relentless in his attacks on The Miz, so much so that the rookie defeated the veteran, humiliating The Miz in the process.

3. Battle to be champion

Night of Champions, **September 19, 2010:**
For months, The Miz—with the help of his new NXT rookie Alex Riley—and Bryan, interfered in each other's matches. Their actions built up to a match for The Miz's United States Championship at *Night of Champions*. Bryan won the Championship by overpowering The Miz and forcing him to submit to the Yes Lock submission hold.

4. Out-of-ring rivalry

Hell in a Cell, **October 3, 2010:** Bryan defended the United States Championship against both The Miz and John Morrison in a Submissions Count Anywhere Match. The three Superstars fought all over the arena. Bryan was able to keep his Championship by forcing The Miz to tap out to the Yes Lock hold on the entrance stage. It would be the last physical confrontation the two would have for eight years, as Daniel Bryan was forced to retire because of injury.

DID YOU KNOW?

On a heated August 23, 2016 edition of *Talking Smack*, Bryan called The Miz a coward, causing The Miz to verbally unload on Bryan, calling him the real coward.

> **"Do you think Daniel Bryan deserves to even be in the same ring as me? Well, I don't."**
>
> NXT, February 23, 2010

5. Renewed rivalry

SummerSlam, **August 19, 2018:**
For two years, Bryan served as the General Manager of *SmackDown Live*. All the while, The Miz mocked Bryan for having to retire. However, in March of 2018, Bryan announced he'd been medically cleared to return to the ring. He soon set his sights on The Miz. The two had the first match at *SummerSlam*. The match looked to be moving in Bryan's favor, but The Miz used brass knuckles to knock Bryan out and win the match. Bryan swore revenge and their rivalry looked set to continue.

BIG SHOW
VS.
MARK HENRY

> **"Mark Henry, all the pain you caused me, I'm going to repay you ten times over."**
> *SmackDown,* October 7, 2011

Big Show's size gives him a solid case for his claim that he is "The World's Largest Athlete." Mark Henry has equally earned the title "The World's Strongest Man" by winning countless weightlifting and strongman competitions, including competing at the Summer Olympics Games. When these two collide, their aggression, bad attitudes, and sheer power create incredible moments and even, on occasion, literal explosions!

383lbs (174kg)

1. Poking the bear

SmackDown, **June 27, 2011:** Mark Henry was set to face his sometimes-friend Big Show in a match, but Show was in a foul mood, and warned Henry not to go through with the match. When Henry ignored that warning, Show attacked him before the match could even begin. In the weeks that followed, both Superstars attacked each other backstage, the violence growing with each encounter.

2. Breaking point

Money in the Bank, **July 17, 2011:** Show and Henry set out to settle their differences in the ring. The mammoth competitors slugged it out, with Henry showcasing an impressive amount of strength by bodyslamming Show. After the match, Henry brutally beat Show with a chair, breaking Show's leg and putting him out of action for three months.

3. Total destruction

Vengeance, **October 23, 2011:** Upon his recovery from his broken leg, Show wanted revenge, and there was no better place than the *Vengeance* pay-per-view. The match ended in a no-contest draw; however, it was still memorable. When Henry suplexed Show from the top rope, both behemoths were sent crashing to the mat. The impact (and their size) caused the ring to collapse.

DISTRUSTED PARTNERS

Show and Henry were an occasional tag team, though they deeply distrusted each other, with good reason.

SmackDown (August 16, 2013) Mark Henry and Big Show teamed with Rob Van Dam to defeat The Shield.

SmackDown (August 8, 2014) Mark Henry and Big Show teamed up to defeat Ryback and Curt Axel, a.k.a. RybAxel.

RAW (October 27, 2014) Mark Henry and Big Show were facing the brother-duo of Goldust and Stardust, when, partway through the match, Henry attacked Big Show, causing them to lose the match and put an end to their partnership.

360lbs (163.29kg)

DID YOU KNOW?

Eventually putting their differences aside, Big Show inducted Mark Henry into the WWE Hall of Fame on April 6, 2018.

4. To the chairs

***TLC: Tables, Ladders, and Chairs*,
December 18, 2011:** Two months after their ring-destroying fight at *Vengeance*, Henry and Show once again faced each other, this time in a Chairs Match. The use of chairs as weapons had particular resonance after Henry's use of one to break Big Show's leg less than six months earlier. The two giants smacked each other with the chairs, wounding but not defeating the other. Show landed a giant punch to Henry's jaw, knocking Henry out and getting the win.

"You have no idea what I'm capable of, Big Show."

SmackDown, July 16, 2011

5. Final face-off

RAW, **November 3, 2014:** Show and Henry had mostly moved on from fighting each other, but three years after their last clash, they renewed the rivalry on *RAW*. Show felt Henry had betrayed him in a tag team match the week before. In a show of strength, Henry put an end to their rivalry by slamming Show onto the steel ring steps. However, he lost the match when he chose to walk away from his rival for good.

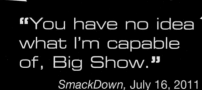

RIVAL FACTS

- Show is recognized as a four-time WWE World Heavyweight Champion; Henry is a one-time World Heavyweight Champion.

- Henry and Show were both ECW Champion once.

CM PUNK
VS.
JOHN CENA

For many years, John Cena had been the face of WWE. He appeared in movies, TV shows, and sold more merchandise than any other WWE Superstar. Another Superstar resented Cena's mainstream success, however. CM Punk was angry all the time and especially when it came to Cena. Punk wanted to take Cena down a couple of notches and prove that he, not Cena, was the best WWE had to offer.

DID YOU KNOW?

Punk and Cena were opponents in the semifinals of the 2009 WWE Superstar of the Year Tournament. Cena won that match.

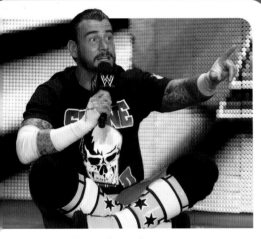

1. Punk pipes up

RAW, **June 27, 2011:** After attacking John Cena and costing him a victory in a Tables Match, CM Punk sat on the entryway and unloaded a verbal tirade he called a Pipe Bomb against WWE Champion Cena, WWE, and the WWE Universe. Threatening that he would win the WWE Championship and defend it in other sports entertainment companies, Punk declared he was the best Superstar in the world.

2. WWE Championship

Money in the Bank, **July 17, 2011:** Punk had a WWE Championship match against Cena and he was determined to win. To complicate matters, Punk's WWE contract was expiring at the end of the night. In front of a riotous crowd, Punk upset the odds and won the Championship, leaving WWE with the Title.

3. Two champs, one title

SummerSlam, **August 14, 2011:** Once Punk left with the WWE Championship, a tournament was held to crown a replacement champion. Cena won the tournament and became WWE Champion. Punk returned from self-imposed exile claiming to be the real WWE Champion since he'd never been beaten. A match between the two Champions was held at *SummerSlam*. Punk won the match, unifying the two Championships.

RIVAL FACTS

● Cena has won a record 16 WWE Championships; Punk won five WWE Championships.

● Punk won and cashed in two Money in the Bank briefcases (2008 and 2009); Cena won the 2012 Money in the Bank contract but was unsuccessful when cashing it in against Punk.

4. Double pin

Night of Champions, **September 16, 2012:** Cena had unsuccessfully tried cashing in his Money in the Bank contract on WWE Champion CM Punk. *RAW* General Manager AJ Lee gave him a second chance at the *Night of Champions* pay-per-view. Punk and Cena both had moments controlling the match. In the end, the two evenly matched Superstars pinned each other at the same time, resulting in a double-pin draw.

"You want to see phony, Punk? Look in the mirror."

RAW, August 8, 2011

5. No walking away

RAW, **November 12, 2012:** With special referee Mick Foley, WWE Champion Punk and Cena faced each other in a non-title match prior to their Triple Threat Match six days later at the *Survivor Series* pay-per-view. After taking a severe beating from Cena, Punk tried to walk away. Cena grabbed him and gave him an Attitude Adjustment slam to get the win.

THE AUTHORITY
VS.
DANIEL BRYAN

Stephanie McMahon and her husband Triple H, collectively known as The Authority, shaped the careers and controlled the destinies of all the Superstars. The Authority wanted to craft the public image of WWE and unkempt Superstars such as Daniel Bryan were an embarrassment. Hoping to drive him away, The Authority abused and attacked Bryan any way they could. But Bryan fought back.

> **"Daniel, you might not be an A, but you're a B+. A solid B+."**
> —Stephanie McMahon,
> *RAW*, August 19, 2013

1. Bad for the image

RAW, **August 5, 2013:** WWE Champion John Cena had hand-picked Daniel Bryan to be his opponent at the upcoming *SummerSlam* event. The Authority didn't like the choice because they felt Bryan didn't represent WWE enough. The Authority tried to get Bryan to clean up his appearance with a haircut or shave and act like a main event star. Bryan flatly rejected their orders.

2. Title snatcher

SummerSlam, **August 18, 2013:** Bryan got his chance at the WWE Championship against Cena. The only problem was that The Authority's Triple H was the special referee. Bryan defeated Cena to win the WWE Championship; however, before he could celebrate the victory, Triple H hit Bryan with his Pedigree slam. Authority member Randy Orton raced to the ring and cashed in his Money in the Bank contract to steal the WWE Championship from Bryan.

3. Ripped off again!

Night of Champions, September 15, 2013: By defeating several opponents sent by The Authority over the previous weeks, Bryan received a WWE Championship Match against Randy Orton. Bryan used his superior in-ring technical skills to pin Orton and win the WWE Championship once again. However, Bryan was immediately stripped of the Title by The Authority, who claimed the referee had counted the pin incorrectly.

TARGETING BRIE BELLA

The Authority found an especially devious way to "punish" and antagonize Daniel Bryan—by focusing on his Superstar wife Brie Bella. After Bryan won the WWE Championship at *WrestleMania XXX*, The Authority ordered him to relinquish the Championship or Brie would be fired. To protect her husband's Title, Brie quit instead. Brie came back at 2014's *SummerSlam* to compete against Stephanie McMahon, but lost when her twin sister Nikki interfered on Stephanie's behalf.

4. Occupying *RAW*

RAW, March 10, 2014: The Authority had employed all kinds of tricks to prevent Bryan from regaining the WWE Championship, so Bryan made it clear: he wanted Triple H in the ring. Triple H refused, until Bryan took his case to the WWE Universe and they joined him in "occupying" *RAW*. Bryan and friends stayed in the ring until Triple H agreed to the match. Furthermore, if Bryan could beat Triple H, he'd be added to the WWE Championship Match at *WrestleMania*.

> "Triple H, if you expect me to back down, I am not going to. I am going to fight!"
>
> *RAW,* March 10, 2014

DID YOU KNOW?

Daniel Bryan and the Authority's Director of Operations, Kane, were once a championship-winning tag team called Team Hell No.

5. Ultimate victory

WrestleMania XXX, April 6, 2014: Bryan and Triple H were the first match at *WrestleMania XXX*. The underdog, Bryan, fought harder than he ever had in his career and beat Triple H. After the match, Stephanie McMahon and Triple H attacked Bryan, hoping to prevent him from winning the WWE Championship later that night. Despite their efforts, Bryan defeated Batista and Randy Orton to become the WWE World Heavyweight Champion.

KEVIN OWENS
VS.
SAMI ZAYN

Sami Zayn and Kevin Owens have known each for a long time. They both grew up in Quebec, Canada, where they trained for sports entertainment careers together. They traveled around the world competing in Mexico, Japan, Australia, and North America, sometimes as partners, sometimes as adversaries. They knew each other so well, that there seemed to be no way to prove a clear victor in their long bitter rivalry.

THE BREAKUP

1. NXT explosion

After years honing their craft around the world, both Sami Zayn and Kevin Owens joined WWE on the NXT brand. At *NXT TakeOver: R Evolution* in 2014, Zayn won the NXT Championship. Owens came to the ring seemingly to celebrate with his boyhood friend, but instead brutally attacked him. Owens defeated Zayn for the NXT Championship two months later, when the referee declared Zayn unable to continue because of the beating Owens

2. Each other's shadow

Royal Rumble, **January 24, 2016:** Owens left NXT for WWE's main roster in mid-2015. Six months later, Zayn debuted in WWE, entering the 30-man Royal Rumble Match and eliminating Owens. In the ensuing weeks, Zayn and Owens attacked each other in the ring, backstage, and during interviews on *RAW* and *SmackDown*. No matter where each of them went, the other always showed up.

3. Turning the tables

Payback, May 1, 2016: After months of clashes, Zayn and Owens finally faced each other in a match. Fists flew and kicks hit home, but ultimately, Owens was able to land his Pop-up Powerbomb on Zayn for the win. Owens celebrated by sitting at the commentary table for the match that followed. However, Zayn attacked again, and officials had to pull them apart.

4. Battle rejoined

Battleground, July 24, 2016: Two months after their showdown at *Payback,* Owens and Zayn went at it again. Owens hit several of his big moves on Zayn, including his Pop-up Powerbomb, his flying dive Frog Splash, and more. Owens implored Zayn to stay down and give up, but Zayn refused to surrender. Zayn hit Owens with several big kicks and massive suplexes to score the victory.

THE MAKEUP

> **"Kevin, I'm going to beat the hell out of you."**
>
> *NXT,* January 28, 2015

5. A dramatic reunion

Just over a year later, at *Hell in a Cell* in October 2017, Owens was facing Shane McMahon in a brutal Hell in a Cell Cage Match. Just as McMahon was about to dive on Owens from the top of the cage, Zayn appeared and moved Owens out of the way. From that night on, the two Superstars were once again partners and friends, helping each other achieve goals in WWE.

RIVAL FACTS

● Owens and Zayn were both NXT Champion for one reign apiece.

● Owens has won several titles in WWE, while Zayn has yet to win one.

CHRIS JERICHO

vs.

CM PUNK

Although they were a generation apart, CM Punk and Chris Jericho followed similar paths to WWE. They both competed all over the world before joining WWE. They were both champions everywhere they competed. They both rose to the top of the mountain in WWE to become multi-time World Heavyweight Champions. And they both called themselves "The best in the world." They competed against each other for the sole purpose of proving who was truly the best.

1. Imposter syndrome

RAW, January 30, 2012:
WWE Champion CM Punk and World Heavyweight Champion Daniel Bryan were embroiled in a match when Chris Jericho raced to the ring to viciously attack Punk. The following week on *RAW,* Jericho berated Punk for being a cheap imitation of him, calling out that Punk referred to himself as "The best in the world," a variation of Jericho's own catchphrase "Best in the world at what I do."

2. End of the world

WrestleMania XXVIII, April 1, 2012: In the weeks after his attack on Punk, Jericho made their issues extremely personal by revealing secrets about Punk's family's past. Jericho warned that their WWE Championship Match at *WrestleMania XXVIII* would be the end of the world. Complicating things, if Punk got disqualified, he would lose the Title. However, that didn't happen, as Punk used his best in-ring skills to defeat Jericho and retain the Championship.

3. Chicago street fight

Extreme Rules, **April 29, 2012:**
After his loss at *WrestleMania XXVIII*, Jericho continued to attack Punk. He even poured alcohol on Punk—grossly offensive to Punk, as he didn't drink. The pair faced off for the WWE Championship in a Chicago Street Fight in Punk's hometown of Chicago. After hitting each other with chairs, tables, and kendo sticks, Punk slammed Jericho into his knee with his Go To Sleep signature move to win the match and keep the Title.

4. Vote of confidence

RAW, **February 4, 2013:**
RAW Management Consultant Booker T ordered Punk into a match where his opponent was voted for by the WWE Universe. They chose Jericho. Punk had lost the WWE Championship to The Rock the night before and was not in the best place mentally. But he focused his efforts and defeated Jericho yet again.

> "Chris, I'm the best wrestler in the world."
>
> *RAW,* February 27, 2012

RIVAL FACTS

- Punk was a five-time WWE World Heavyweight Champion; Jericho was one better as a six-time Champion.

- Jericho holds the record for most reigns as Intercontinental Champion with nine; Punk won that Title only once.

- Jericho conceived the Money in the Bank Match, but never won it; however, Punk won it twice in back-to-back years, in 2008 and 2009.

- Jericho is a nine-time Tag Team Champion in WWE; Punk was a one-time Tag Team Champion.

5. Hometown hero

Payback, **June 16, 2013:** Punk had taken a couple of months off from WWE after a grueling reign as WWE Champion. Jericho mocked Punk's absence, challenging him to a match at *Payback*. Punk's friend Paul Heyman accepted the match, which would be back in Punk's hometown of Chicago. Jericho and Punk used their full arsenal of moves against each other, but Punk won what would be the final match between the rivals.

JOHN CENA VS. THE MIZ

John Cena and The Miz may not admit it, but they are alike in many ways. They have both been WWE Champion, headlined *WrestleMania*, and are passionate about WWE. But they really, really don't like each other. Cena views The Miz as a boasting, delusional jerk. The Miz thinks Cena doesn't respect him at all (and he's probably not wrong about that). Whenever they come to blows, it's a must-see event.

"Miz, you're not the Undertaker, but if you press me again, you're a dead man."

SmackDown, February 28, 2017

1. Rockin' time

WrestleMania XXVII, April 3, 2011: It all started when John Cena won an Elimination Chamber Match to win a title opportunity against The Miz at *WrestleMania XXVII*. Their disdain for one another reached a boiling point leading into the match. They fought to a double-count-out draw, but the *WrestleMania* host, The Rock, ordered the match restarted. The Rock then interfered, attacking Cena and allowing Miz to get the win.

2. Cena's revenge

Extreme Rules, May 1, 2011: Less than a month after *WrestleMania XXVII*, Cena got another chance at The Miz's WWE Title. This time, the match occurred inside a steel cage with Superstar John Morrison, who had won the chance to be included in the match. Regardless of Morrison's presence, it was all about Cena and Miz. The match ended when Cena gave Miz an Attitude Adjustment slam off the top rope to win the WWE Championship.

3. No cheating

Over the Limit, **May 22, 2011:** The Miz demanded his rematch against Cena for the WWE Championship take place three weeks after Extreme Rules at *Over the Limit.* Cena announced their match would be an "I Quit" Match. During the match, The Miz used a recording of John Cena saying "I quit" to seemingly win, but the referee discovered the deception and restarted the contest. Cena used his STF submission hold to force The Miz to quit, winning the match.

4. Imitation games

SmackDown, **February 28, 2017:** Following their "I Quit" Match, Cena and The Miz moved on to other rivalries. But in February 2017, The Miz and his wife Maryse criticized Cena for being too powerful on their talk show, Miz TV. Maryse slapped Cena, so Cena's girlfriend Nikki Bella attacked Maryse. In the weeks that followed, Miz and Maryse made skits mocking Cena and Bella's appearance on the reality TV show *Total Bellas.*

TEAMMATES... FOR A MINUTE

During the February 21, 2011 episode of *RAW,* John Cena and The Miz were ordered to compete together as a tag team, despite the fact they were going to be opponents at *WrestleMania XXVII* six weeks later. Their opponents were Heath Slater and Justin Gabriel of The CORRE faction, who also happened to be WWE Tag Team Champions. Cena and Miz set aside their differences for the sake of their impromptu team and won the match and Tag Team Championship together. Immediately after the match, The CORRE invoked their automatic rematch clause, allowing them to challenge for the Tag Team Championship. The CORRE won back the Championship by pinning Cena after The Miz revived their old rivalry and suddenly attacked Cena.

"Cena, your shirt says 'Respect, Earn It,' well, I've been earning it for twelve years!"

RAW, August 21, 2017

5. Mixed result

WrestleMania 33, **April 2, 2017:** Disgusted by the parodies The Miz and Maryse had made of them, Cena and Bella challenged them to a Mixed Tag Team Match at *WrestleMania 33.* Cena and Bella teamed up and hit their signature moves on The Miz and Maryse, pinning both for the win and putting an end to the rivalry.

CHARLOTTE FLAIR

VS.

SASHA BANKS

Charlotte Flair and Sasha Banks were considered the most athletic, talented female in-ring performers in NXT, where they both started their careers. The two Superstars were sometimes friends and allies, but a fierce competitive streak ran through their time at NXT and their fight for the NXT Women's Championship. This competitiveness only grew when they joined WWE, when each sought the *RAW* Women's Championship.

"To be the woman, you've got to beat the woman!"

SmackDown, June 23, 2016

1. NXT steps

RAW, July 13, 2015: In a new era for WWE, co-owner Stephanie McMahon declared it was time for the women of WWE to shine in a Women's Revolution. Banks and Flair both debuted as part of this Revolution. Flair had not gotten over her NXT Title loss to Banks, and the former friends leaped at the chance to renew their rivalry on a new stage.

2. Trading titles

RAW, **July 25, 2016:** Rising quickly through the ranks, Flair had won the Diva's Championship in September 2015 and remained champ for an impressive 10 months, during which the Title was renamed the WWE Women's Championship. However, Banks defeated Flair on this edition of *RAW*, just as she had in NXT. Banks' reign as Champion didn't last long, as Flair recaptured the Title a month later at *SummerSlam*.

Hell in a Cell, October 30, 2016: Flair and Banks made history when they became the first women to compete in a Cell Match at *Hell in a Cell* in 2016. The match spilled outside the ring, and both women used the cage walls as a weapon. Flair won the match and the Women's Championship that was at stake.

Before joining WWE, Charlotte Flair and Sasha Banks had many epic matches for the NXT Women's Championship. Here are four of the best.

NXT TakeOver: R Evolution (December 11, 2014) NXT Women's Champion Flair retained the Title against Banks, escalating a recent falling-out.

NXT (December 25, 2014) In a Christmas Day rematch, Flair was again successful in defending the Title against a furious Banks.

NXT TakeOver: Rival (February 11, 2015) In a rare Fatal 4-Way Match, Banks won against Flair, Becky Lynch, and Bayley to become the new NXT Women's Champion.

NXT (July 15, 2015) Banks successfully defended the NXT Women's Championship one last time against Flair.

> **"There is no queen in WWE, but there is a Boss!"**
>
> *RAW*, October 24, 2016

4. Open season

RAW, **November 28, 2016:** In retaliation, Banks challenged Flair for the Title in a Falls Count Anywhere Match. With no rules, Flair and Banks used canes, the ringside barricade, steel posts, and more to inflict pain on each other. They even fought their way through the crowd. Banks eventually threaded her opponent through a handrail on the arena stairs and locked her in her Bank Statement submission hold to win the Championship.

5. Iron woman

Roadblock: End of the Line, December 18, 2016: Banks and Flair competed in their final match against each other at the end of 2016. It was a 30-minute Iron Man Match, where whoever got more victories in half an hour would be declared Champion. At the end of the allotted time, they were tied 2-2. Flair won the final pin in sudden death overtime, proving her dominance over Banks.

RIVAL FACTS

● Flair is a six-time Women's Champion, with Banks one Championship win behind her rival.

● Both Banks and Flair have held the NXT Women's Championship once.

BROCK LESNAR

VS.

UNDERTAKER

"The Beast" Brock Lesnar is one of WWE's most dominant figures, and has been for many years. But there's one Superstar who has had an even longer tenure in WWE and dominated, not just for years, but decades: Undertaker. They are both monstrous, cold-blooded Superstars who are experts at inflicting pain and punishment on their opponents. When their paths cross, those efforts are increased to match the hatred they have for each other.

DID YOU KNOW?
Undertaker and Lesnar's rivalry went beyond WWE. The pair had words following one of Lesnar's UFC Championship fights in 2010.

6ft 3in (1.90m)

1. The contract
RAW, **February 24, 2014:** Brock Lesnar had an open contract for any opponent to face him at *WrestleMania XXX*. Undertaker, who was defending a 21-match winning streak at *WrestleMania,* was glad to sign the contract. Undertaker gave Lesnar a Chokeslam through a table and stared at the *WrestleMania XXX* sign hanging high in the arena. Lesnar accepted the implied challenge, determined to end Undertaker's streak.

2. Breaking the streak
WrestleMania 30, **April 6, 2014:** In the weeks leading up to *WrestleMania XXX*, Lesnar and his manager Paul Heyman swore they would end Undertaker's streak. No one believed them. However, the WWE Universe was stunned when, after giving Undertaker three of his F-5 slams, Lesnar succeeded in his goal.

3. Shocking return

Battleground, July 19, 2015:
Undertaker had mostly disappeared from WWE after losing to Lesnar at *WrestleMania XXX*. Lesnar, meanwhile, had won and lost the WWE Championship since their encounter. Lesnar was competing for the WWE Championship against Seth Rollins at *Battleground* when Undertaker shockingly returned to WWE and attacked him, costing him the WWE Championship.

6ft 10in
(2.08m)

4. Mutual revenge

SummerSlam, August 23, 2015:
Brock Lesnar and Undertaker would have their next chance at each other at *SummerSlam*. After an intense fight, Lesnar locked on his Kimura Lock submission hold. The ringside timekeeper thought Undertaker had submitted and rang the bell. The referee hadn't seen the submission and restarted the match. Undertaker hit Lesnar below the belt and locked on his Hell's Gate submission, forcing Lesnar to pass out. The referee awarded Undertaker the match.

> **"Lesnar, the hounds of Hell are baying for your soul, and the gates of Hell are opening for you."**
>
> *RAW,* August 17, 2015

THE EARLIER YEARS

More than a decade before their rivalry surrounding Undertaker's *WrestleMania* streak, Brock Lesnar and Undertaker competed in a series of matches for the WWE Championship.

Unforgiven (September 22, 2002) Lesnar retained the WWE Championship when he and Undertaker were both disqualified.

No Mercy (October 20, 2002) As they would nearly 15 years later, Undertaker and WWE Champion Lesnar battled inside the Hell in a Cell steel cage. And just as would occur in the future, Lesnar used his F-5 to defeat Undertaker inside the Cell.

No Mercy (October 19, 2003) WWE Champion Lesnar retained the WWE Championship in a Biker Chain Match, in which a steel chain hanging high above the ring can be used as a weapon. Lesnar seized the chain, thanks to help from Mr. McMahon, and won.

5. To hell and back

Hell in a Cell, October 25, 2015:
After the controversial ending to their *SummerSlam* match, Lesnar and Undertaker agreed to fight one another inside the giant Hell in a Cell steel cage. Taking a beating from Undertaker, Lesnar pulled the mat off the ring, exposing the metal and wood beneath it. After hitting Undertaker with three F-5 slams on the wood, Lesnar won, proving his dominance once and for all.

DEAN AMBROSE
VS.
SETH ROLLINS

Dean Ambrose and Seth Rollins know each other better than perhaps any other Superstars. They traveled around the world together, competing in sports entertainment and building their careers in NXT. They were brothers in arms in their faction, The Shield. They knew every detail about each other, including their secrets and tricks. This knowledge served each of them well when they entered into a long rivalry with one another.

THE BREAKUP

"Everybody knows somebody like you, Seth. The kind of guy who stabs his brother in the back ...."

RAW, June 9, 2014

1. Broken Shield

For two years, The Shield had been the dominant faction in WWE. But when Seth Rollins, the "Architect" of The Shield, decided to pursue his individual championship goals alone, the group began to splinter. On the June 2, 2014 episode of *RAW*, Rollins attacked his Shield brethren Roman Reigns and Dean Ambrose, ending the group and earning him Ambrose's lasting ire.

2. Lumberjack match

SummerSlam, August 17, 2014: Over the summer of 2014, Rollins and Ambrose attacked each other whenever they could. To try to settle their differences, they battled in a Lumberjack Match at *SummerSlam* with other Superstars surrounding the ring. During a chaotic match where the surrounding Lumberjacks fought among themselves, Rollins used his metal *Money in the Bank* briefcase to hit Ambrose and get the win.

Over the three years of their rivalry, Rollins and Ambrose fought for the WWE World Heavyweight Championship in many matches.

Elimination Chamber (May 31, 2015) Ambrose won by disqualification when Rollins used the referee as a shield from Ambrose's attack. However, Ambrose didn't win the Championship due to the disqualification.

Money in the Bank (June 15, 2015) Rollins retained the WWE Championship in a Ladder Match by climbing a ladder and retrieving the Title before Ambrose.

RAW (July 18, 2016) Ambrose retained the Title when their match ended in a draw because of a double pin.

3. Cell mates

Hell in a Cell, October 26, 2014: After causing The Shield to crumble, Rollins had joined Triple H's stable of Superstars called The Authority. Ambrose was desperate to get another chance to face Rollins. To do so, he had to jump through many of The Authority's hoops, like defeating John Cena in a match. Finally, Ambrose faced Rollins in a Hell in a Cell Match. During the match, several members of The Authority—including Kane, J & J Security, and Bray Wyatt—all attacked Ambrose, securing Rollins the win.

4. Peak rivalry

Money in the Bank, June 19, 2016: For the next two years, Rollins and Ambrose battled each other all over the world. Rollins won the WWE Championship, which Ambrose stole and pretended he was Champion. The height of their rivalry came at 2016's *Money in the Bank* event. Rollins had won his WWE Championship at the main event, but his reign did not last. Ambrose had won a Money in the Bank Championship Match contract earlier that night. He immediately cashed it in and defeated Rollins in eight seconds.

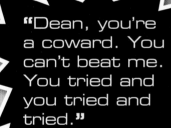

> "Dean, you're a coward. You can't beat me. You tried and you tried and tried."
>
> *RAW*, July 11, 2016

THE MAKEUP

5. Reunited

A year after the *Money in the Bank* cash-in, Ambrose was being attacked by *RAW* Tag Team Champions Sheamus and Ceasaro when Rollins raced to the ring to make the save. On the August 14, 2017 episode of *RAW*, Ambrose and Rollins fought off another attack from Ceasaro and Sheamus, and celebrated with a Shield fist bump. A week later at *SummerSlam*, they won the *RAW* Tag Team Championship together.

RIVAL FACTS

● Rollins is a two-time WWE World Heavyweight Champion. Ambrose beat Rollins for his one and only WWE Championship win.

● Ambrose is a two-time Intercontinental Champion, while Rollins has held that Title once.

● Rollins and Ambrose both won the *Money in the Bank* match once—Rollins in 2014, Ambrose in 2016.

AJ LEE
VS.
PAIGE

Paige and AJ Lee had a complicated relationship. They competed over the Divas Championship, and that competition stoked flames of anger between them. However, they also professed to be best friends. But was their friendship real? Maybe not at first, but the more they competed in the ring, the more authentic their friendship became, and they grew to watch out for each other like true friends do.

"I don't play little girl games, Paige. If I have a problem with you, it'll be to your face, like a real woman!"

RAW, July 28, 2014

THE BREAKUP

1. Out of the blue

AJ Lee had successfully defended her WWE Divas Championship at *WrestleMania XXX.* The following night was the April 7, 2014 edition of *RAW.* Lee was celebrating her victory when she was challenged to a match by NXT Women's Champion Paige, who was making her WWE debut. Lee accepted and moments later, Paige defeated Lee—ending Lee's, at the time, record-setting Divas Championship reign.

2. Surprise return

RAW, **June 30, 2014:** Lee disappeared for nearly three months after losing the Divas Championship to Paige. When she unexpectedly returned to *RAW,* she copied Paige's approach and challenged Paige to an impromptu match. Paige hesitantly accepted, and just as Paige had done to her, Lee quickly won back the Divas Championship with a decisive victory.

4. Last defense

Hell in a Cell, October 26, 2014: The Divas Championship had changed hands again one month earlier at the *Night of Champions* pay-per-view, with Lee once again victorious. In what would be their final match against each other, the pair battle with everything they had. This time, Lee was able to lock in her Black Widow hold, forcing Paige to tap out. Lee retained the Title that day, but would lose it to Nikki Bella just a month later.

3. Friendly attacks

SummerSlam, August 17, 2014: Following Lee's shock return and Title win, she and Paige pretended to be close friends. However, while publicly acting like friends, they would attack each other backstage. This conflict led to a *SummerSlam* match. Paige countered Lee's Black Widow submission hold, turned it into a Ram-Paige slam, and got the win to once again become Divas Champion.

DID YOU KNOW?

The Paige/Lee rivalry is told as part of the 2019 feature film *Fighting With My Family* produced by WWE Studios.

> "Roses are red, woodchips are beige. I'm sorry I pushed you right off the stage. It's not like I hate you. I like you a bunch. But you just have that face that I want to punch."
>
> *RAW, August 11, 2014*

THE MAKEUP

5. Making the save

After losing the Title to Nikki Bella, Lee took time off from WWE. She returned on the March 2, 2015 edition of *RAW* and saved Paige from an attack by the Bella Twins, who had been targeting Paige during Lee's absence. Now on the same side, Paige and Lee challenged the Bellas to a tag team match at *WrestleMania 31*, which they won. Lee retired from WWE a few days later, closing this chapter in her and Paige's careers.

RIVAL FACTS

- Lee was a three-time Divas Champion; Paige held the Title twice.

- Paige was the only Superstar to hold the NXT Women's Championship and WWE Divas Championship simultaneously.

DOLPH ZIGGLER
VS.
THE MIZ

The Miz is an arrogant, narcissistic Superstar who believes he's the greatest addition to sports entertainment in history. Dolph Ziggler is confident to the point of cocky, a brash Superstar who wants to be remembered as the best athlete ever to compete in WWE. Similar in size and skill, they are evenly matched in the ring, so when these two giant personalities and egos clash, the collision is always colossally entertaining.

6ft (1.82m)

1. Switching champs

SummerSlam, **August 17, 2014:** One month earlier, The Miz had won a Battle Royal to win the vacant Intercontinental Championship. His first challenger was set to be Dolph Ziggler at *SummerSlam*. Their back-and-forth contest ended when Ziggler hit his signature Zig-Zag move, slamming The Miz to the mat and pinning him for a three count. Ziggler became the new Intercontinental Champion.

2. Two illegal pins

Night of Champions and *RAW*, **September 21 and 22, 2014:** The Miz received a rematch against Dolph Ziggler one month later at *Night of Champions*. The Miz successfully recaptured the Intercontinental Championship by rolling his rival up in a pin and illegally holding on to Ziggler's tights. However, the next night on *RAW,* The Miz lost the Championship back to Ziggler, when Ziggler got his own back, rolling up Miz and illegally holding on to his tights.

"No one will ever believe in you, Miz ... You want to prove yourself, fight me."

SmackDown, August 30, 2016

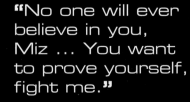

- Dolph Ziggler is a two-time WWE World Heavyweight Champion; The Miz has held the WWE Championship once.

- The Miz is an eight-time Intercontinental Champion; Dolph Ziggler is a six-time Intercontinental Champion.

3. Taunts and tricks

***Backlash*, September 11, 2016:** The next really significant encounter between The Miz and Dolph Ziggler occured at *Backlash* in 2016. The Miz had been insulting *SmackDown* General Manager Daniel Bryan over Bryan's forced retirement due to injury. Bryan convinced Ziggler to represent him and challenge Miz for the Intercontinental Championship. However, The Miz retained his Title when his wife, Maryse, sprayed pepper spray in Ziggler's eyes.

6ft 2in (1.87m)

> "Ziggler, all you ever do is lose. You're the biggest loser I've ever seen."
>
> *Main Event,*
> November 12, 2014

4. Kicking back

***No Mercy*, October 9, 2016:** Desperate to get revenge on The Miz for his wife's pepper spray attack, Dolph Ziggler put his career on the line against The Miz's Intercontinental Championship. If Ziggler couldn't win the Title, he'd retire. Ziggler's desperation was a powerful motivator as he hit The Miz with his signature Superkick to win the Championship and save his career.

5. A future rematch?

***TLC: Tables, Ladders, and Chairs*, December 4, 2016:** On the November 15 edition of *SmackDown Live*, The Miz had won the Intercontinental Championship back from Ziggler. Ziggler promptly challenged The Miz to a Ladder Match, where the Title hung above the ring. The first Superstar to grab it would win. The Miz fought dirty throughout and retrieved the Title for the win. The WWE Universe eagerly await the day Ziggler has another shot at The Miz.

THE SHIELD
vs.
THE WYATT FAMILY

The Shield—Roman Reigns, Dean Ambrose, and Seth Rollins—called themselves the "Hounds of Justice" because they tried to enforce what they felt was right. The Wyatt Family, including Bray Wyatt, Luke Harper, and Erick Rowan, aimed to inflict punishment on those around them. This conflict of ideals set The Shield and The Wyatt Family on a collision course.

1. Costly attack

RAW, January 27, 2014: The Shield was embroiled in a match against John Cena, Sheamus, and Daniel Bryan, with the winning team's members being entered into the upcoming Elimination Chamber Match for the WWE Championship. The Wyatt Family deliberately sabotaged the match by attacking John Cena. This caused The Shield to be disqualified, costing them the match and their opportunity at the WWE Championship.

BRAY VS. ROMAN

In addition to the two teams facing each other, their leaders, Bray Wyatt and Roman Reigns, have battled one-on-one many times.

RAW (September 28, 2015) Roman Reigns slammed Bray Wyatt through the announcers' table, causing a no-contest draw.

RAW (May 22, 2017) The match between Wyatt and Reigns ended in a no-contest draw when Samoa Joe attacked both Superstars.

RAW (June 5, 2017) Reigns crushed Wyatt, pausing their rivalry for more than six months.

RAW (February 5, 2018) Reigns defeated Wyatt to win a spot in the Elimination Chamber Match three weeks later.

2. The Hounds and the haunted

Elimination Chamber, February 23, 2014: Livid over their loss on *RAW*, The Shield demanded a match against The Wyatt Family at the *Elimination Chamber* pay-per-view. All six Superstars fought with great hatred for their opponents. They brawled through the crowd and all over the arena. The match ended when Bray Wyatt executed his Sister Abigail move on Reigns, pinning him for the victory.

3. Bad blood

RAW, **March 3, 2014:** The match at Elimination Chamber settled nothing between the two teams. They battled again a week later on *RAW*. Rollins, frustrated by his teammates' mistakes, abandoned them, allowing The Wyatt Family to once again overcome The Shield.

RIVAL FACTS

- The Shield won the WWE Tag Team Championship twice; The Wyatt Family were Tag Team Champions once in NXT and once in WWE.

- Each member of The Shield also won singles championships—the United States and Intercontinental Championships—during their rivalry with The Wyatt Family.

> **"I welcome this war! Bring it to me!"**
>
> —Bray Wyatt, *RAW*, February 4, 2014

4. Victory

Main Event, **April 8, 2014:** One month later, the two teams collided again. For the first time, The Shield was able to get a win over The Wyatt Family thanks to more effective teamwork. Reigns hit Bray with a Superman Punch, Rollins Stomped Harper, and Ambrose leveled Rowan with his Dirty Deeds slam for the win.

5. Getting closure

RAW, **May 5, 2014:** The Wyatt Family engaged with The Shield one more time a month after losing on *Main Event*. Just as The Shield was about to slam Wyatt with a triple powerbomb, the recently reunited Evolution faction, who had their sights set on The Shield, interfered to distract them. The Wyatts capitalized, pinning Reigns for the win. It would be their final match against each other, as both teams split up in the weeks following this match.

CHARLOTTE FLAIR
VS.
NATALYA

It's a collision of legacies when Natalya and Charlotte Flair meet. They are both from legendary families in sports entertainment. Natalya's father Jim "The Anvil" Neidhart was a Tag Team Champion, and she was trained by her Hall of Fame grandfather Stu Hart. Meanwhile, Charlotte Flair is the daughter of 16-time World Champion and two-time Hall of Famer Ric Flair. Both are gifted athletes in their own right who battle for supremacy.

> **"Nattie, my family will always be better than your family."**
> *RAW*, April 4, 2016

1. Women's Revolution

*Roadblock***, March 12, 2016:** Charlotte Flair had come to WWE as part of the Women's Revolution, where female Superstars were being given higher profiles. Charlotte had quickly won the Diva's Championship, and Natalya was upset. She'd been in WWE longer than Charlotte and believed she deserved the respect the newcomer was receiving. Natalya faced Charlotte at *Roadblock*, but was unable to win the Championship.

2. Cheated by you

*Payback***, May 1, 2016:** At *WrestleMania 32* a month earlier, the Divas Championship was retired and Flair won the new WWE Women's Championship that replaced it. When Flair declared her family was superior to Natalya's, a match was set for *Payback*. During the match, Charlotte put Natalya in the Hart family's signature Sharpshooter hold. The referee rang the bell, awarding the match to Charlotte, despite Natalya not submitting, cheating her out of a possible win.

3. Do you submit?

Extreme Rules, May 22, 2016: Three weeks after their showdown at *Payback,* Natalya and Charlotte faced off in a Submission Match, where the only way to win is for the winner to force their opponent to give up. Natalya had put her Sharpshooter hold on Charlotte, when Charlotte's friend Dana Brooke came out dressed as Ric Flair. This distraction caused Natalya to break the hold and allowed Charlotte to put the Figure-Eight Leglock on Natalya to win.

4. Renewed rivalry

SmackDown, November 14, 2017: The 2016 Superstar Draft had meant Natalya and Charlotte weren't competing on the same WWE brand for over a year. In that time, Natalya had secured the *SmackDown* Women's Championship. Once Charlotte was drafted to *SmackDown Live* in 2017, she targeted Natalya's Title. Charlotte successfully won it by once again getting Natalya to submit to her Figure-Eight Leglock.

> **"You keep talking about being genetically superior, but I have the heart of a champion."**
>
> *RAW,* April 4, 2016

5. Totally surrounded

Clash of Champions, **December 17, 2017:** Natalya got a rematch against Charlotte for the *SmackDown* Women's Championship one week later in a Lumberjack Match, where all the female Superstars, called "Lumberjacks," surrounded the ring. Despite most of the Lumberjacks attacking Charlotte during the match, she was able to overcome Natalya to retain the Title. The WWE Universe celebrated with Charlotte, while eagerly looking forward to more encounters between Charlotte and Natalya in the future.

RIVAL FACTS

- Natalya is a one-time Diva's Champion and one-time *SmackDown* Women's Champion.

- Charlotte Flair is a former NXT Women's Champion, Diva's Champion, *SmackDown* Women's Champion, and four-time *RAW* Women's Champion.

BROCK LESNAR VS. ROMAN REIGNS

As a seemingly unstoppable champion, Brock Lesnar was on top of the WWE mountain, right where Roman Reigns wanted to be. Reigns repeatedly challenged Lesnar for the WWE and Universal Championships. As the pair battled each other, their hatred grew. Lesnar thought Reigns was weak, as annoying as a mosquito, and an embarrassment to his family's rich legacy in sports entertainment. Reigns hated Lesnar because he felt the Champion was selfish, lazy, and undeserving of being Champion.

1. Suplex City

WrestleMania 31, **March 29, 2015:** Reigns had earned a match against WWE Champion Lesnar at *WrestleMania 31*. A chance at the Championship was all Reigns wanted, so, although he went into the match feeling like an underdog, he was determined to win. Lesnar used countless German Suplexes to throw Reigns around the ring, but no clear winner was determined, because Superstar Seth Rollins cashed in his Money in the Bank contract to steal the Championship from them both.

2. Four's company

SummerSlam, **August 20, 2017:** Two years after their clash at *WrestleMania 31*, Reigns and Lesnar battled each other again. Lesnar had become WWE Universal Champion and in this match defended the Title against Reigns, as well as Samoa Joe and Braun Strowman in a Fatal 4-Way Match. Lesnar's annoyance with Reigns and Reigns' disgust of Lesnar caused them to focus on each other, all but ignoring the two other opponents. Lesnar gave Reigns his F-5 slam to get the win and remain Champion.

3. Another chance

WrestleMania 34, **April 8, 2018:** By *WrestleMania 34*, Lesnar and Reigns' hatred of each other had reached a boiling point. Reigns was desperate to take the Universal Championship from Lesner. He believed WWE deserved a proud Champion who showed up to defend the Title every week. The pair battled like wild animals, literally pouring blood, sweat, and tears into the struggle. Reigns fought nobly, but in the end succumbed to Lesnar's superior power, losing the match.

> **"Brock Lesnar is an entitled piece of (trash) who hides behind his Championship."**
>
> *RAW,* February 26, 2018

4. Questionable decision

Greatest Royal Rumble, **April 27, 2018:** Three weeks after *WrestleMania 34*, Reigns' eagerness to defeat Lesnar got the better of him during a Steel Cage Match. He speared Lesnar through the cage wall with incredible force, so it appeared to the referee that Lesnar landed first out of the cage. In fact, Reigns had landed outside the cage first and should've therefore been declared the winner. The referee awarded the match to Lesnar, however, letting him keep his Universal Championship.

5. Last struggle?

SummerSlam, **August 19, 2018:** Having held the Universal Championship for over a year and a half, Lesnar seemed unstoppable. He was eyeing a return to UFC and MMA fighting and planned to take the WWE Universal Championship with him. Reigns stood in his way one more time at *SummerSlam*, determined to finally defeat Lesnar and keep the Universal Championship in WWE. To the delight of the WWE Universe, Reigns succeeded, promising to be the fighting Champion the people deserved.

BAYLEY VS. SASHA BANKS

RIVAL FACTS

● Bayley has won both the NXT and *RAW* Women's Championships on one occasion.

● Sasha Banks has won the NXT Championship once and the *RAW* Women's Championship four times.

Growing up watching WWE as little girls, both Sasha Banks and Bayley dreamed of one day entering the ring and becoming WWE Women's Champion. They joined NXT at the same time and frequently competed with each other. Fierce competition initially led to mutual respect and even friendship. But eventually that friendship soured into anger and disdain. Sasha felt she was better than Bayley and Bayley bitterly resented Sasha's attitude.

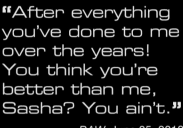

"After everything you've done to me over the years! You think you're better than me, Sasha? You ain't."

RAW, June 25, 2018

DID YOU KNOW?

Together with Charlotte Flair and Becky Lynch, Sasha Banks and Bayley make up the Four Horsewomen of WWE.

1. Bayley's time

NXT TakeOver: Brooklyn, **August 22, 2015:** NXT Women's Champion Sasha Banks had begun to treat Bayley nastily in NXT. She was dismissive and condescending to Bayley, calling her a loser. Always feeling like the underdog, Bayley was determined to prove herself to Banks. They'd traded wins back and forth over the years, but at *NXT TakeOver: Brooklyn*, Bayley finally beat Banks when it mattered: for the NXT Women's Championship.

2. Iron women

NXT TakeOver: Respect, **October 7, 2015:** Banks was granted a rematch against Bayley for the NXT Women's Championship. NXT General Manager William Regal announced this rematch would be the first ever Women's Iron Man Match in WWE history. As with the men's Iron Man matches, the Superstar with the most victories in a set amount of time would win. Bayley won the 30-minute match in the last few seconds, three victories to two.

3. Partners

Battleground, July 24, 2016: For weeks, Sasha Banks had tried to defeat the combined forces of Charlotte Flair and Dana Brooke. Banks was due to face Flair and Brooke in a tag team match at *Battleground*. As the match was about to begin, Banks revealed her partner was Bayley, who was making her WWE main roster debut. Their battles in NXT had brought them together, and they proved they made an effective team with their victory.

INTERVENTION

To get their anger issues under control, *RAW* General Manager Kurt Angle ordered Sasha Banks and Bayley to go to counseling together. Their therapist, Dr. Shelby, had worked with Daniel Bryan and Kane years earlier, resulting in the formation of their championship-winning tag team "Hell No." Just like them, therapy helped Bayley and Banks also form a new tag team, at least temporarily, called The Boss 'n' Hug Connection.

4. Backstabbed

Elimination Chamber, February 25, 2018: Bayley and Banks were two of the seven entrants in the first ever Women's Elimination Chamber match for the *RAW* Women's Championship. The pair had been close friends; however, that was forgotten in the Chamber. While neither one of them won, Sasha shoved Bayley to the mat from high above the ring and pinned her to eliminate her from the match.

> "Bayley, you're a loser! Pathetic! You will never, ever, ever beat me!"
>
> *NXT TakeOver Brooklyn,* August 22, 2015

5. Never enough

RAW, June 25, 2018: Years of pent up frustration and resentment finally exploded in Bayley. After Bank's betrayal at *Elimination Chamber* and continued attacks during matches and backstage, Bayley unloaded on her former friend, pummeling her with harsh fists and even throwing her into the ringside stairs. Although the outburst was satisfying for Bayley, she knew Banks would eventually get revenge, and things would remain as they always did: unresolved.

AJ STYLES
VS.
JOHN CENA

AJ Styles had proven himself to be one of the best in-ring competitors all over the world. His technical skill was unmatched, but he'd never competed in WWE until 2016. He wanted to prove that he was the best, and that meant targeting the best in WWE—John Cena. Cena wasn't worried, having faced countless upstart Superstars. But Styles was no upstart—he was arguably more talented and experienced than anyone Cena had faced before.

THE BREAKUP

1. Beat up John Cena

John Cena had been out of action for five months due to a shoulder injury. He returned to WWE on the May 30, 2016 episode of *RAW*, and was welcomed back by AJ Styles, who congratulated him on an unexpectedly fast recovery before attacking him. He pummeled Cena, bragging later that his new favorite thing to do was "Beat up John Cena."

> "Cena, you know every time you step in the ring with me, you know I'm the better man in it."
>
> *Smackdown Live*, January 24, 2017

2. Club thugs

Money in the Bank, **June 19, 2016:** Styles' attack on Cena led the pair to a match at *Money in the Bank* three weeks later. It was a spectacular display of in-ring offense as both Superstars hit their signature moves and submission holds. After Cena accidentally knocked the referee down, Styles' best friends and stablemates—members of The Club—attacked Cena, and put Styles atop him to get the win.

DID YOU KNOW?

When he defeated Styles for the WWE World Heavyweight Championship, Cena tied Ric Flair's legendary record as a 16-time champion.

3. Trade off

***SummerSlam*, August 21, 2016:** In the Superstar Draft in July, Cena and Styles were both drafted to *SmackDown*. The Club was also split up, allowing Cena and Styles' next match at *SummerSlam* to be a true one-on-one encounter. Once again, both Superstars used their best moves and in-ring attacks against each other. When Cena tried his Attitude Adjustment slam, Styles countered it into his Styles Clash move, pinning Cena for the victory.

4. The champ is here

***Royal Rumble*, January 29, 2017:** In the months following their match at *SummerSlam*, AJ Styles became WWE Champion and John Cena became number one contender. Moves and countermoves were the norm for these two Superstars. However, this time the style and outcome was different from their first two matches, as Cena hit Styles with four Attitude Adjustment slams to win the WWE Championship.

> "Styles, you've been hot for six months. I've held this place down for well over a decade."
>
> *Smackown Live*, January 24, 2017

THE MAKEUP

5. Hustle, loyalty, earned respect

Styles and Cena didn't face each other again for over a year. By this time, Styles had won back the WWE Championship and was set to defend it at *Fastlane* against Cena, Kevin Owens, Sami Zayn, Baron Corbin, and Dolph Ziggler. The Championship was more important to Cena because, if he won, he'd get a match at *WrestleMania 34* two months later. The chaotic match ended when Styles pinned Owens. Afterward, Cena raised Styles' hand in a show of respect, putting an end to their conflict.

CLUB ATTACKS

During his rivalry with Styles, Cena had to contend with Styles' best friends Luke Gallows and Karl Anderson, with whom Styles had formed The Club stable in Japan. The Club reformed in WWE when all three Superstars joined the company.

RAW (June 20, 2016) Cena's match against Karl Anderson ended in a disqualification win for Cena when the full Club attacked him.

SmackDown Live (July 19, 2016) Cena beat Luke Gallows in a one-on-one match after Enzo Amore and Big Cass stopped the Club from interfering.

Battleground (July 24, 2016) Cena teamed with Enzo and Cass to defeat the three members of The Club.

RAW (August 28, 2017) Cena teamed up with Roman Reigns to defeat Gallows and Anderson.

CHRIS JERICHO

VS.

KEVIN OWENS

Growing up near Montreal, Canada, Kevin Owens loved watching WWE. His favorite Superstar was Chris Jericho. In fact, watching Jericho inspired Owens to pursue a career in sports entertainment. Once he joined WWE, Owens was excited to work with Jericho in the ring and get to know him outside the ring. However, this hero worship dissolved over the course of a couple of years into an intense, personal rivalry.

THE LIST OF JERICHO

While teaming with Owens, Jericho created the "List of Jericho," featuring the names of those Superstars who annoyed him and Kevin Owens. Some of the most prominent include:

Gallows and Anderson

The New Day

Seth Rollins

Mick Foley (x3)

Lita

Bray Wyatt

Booker T

Booker T's Hall of Fame Ring

Goldberg

1. The best of friends

Late 2016: Chris Jericho was a legend in WWE, but he sometimes needed help to defeat opponents. On this episode of *RAW,* he found a new ally in Kevin Owens. From then on, Owens and Jericho helped each other to win matches and championships. Owens became Universal Champion and Jericho United States Champion. Tension grew when Jericho accepted a championship challenge from Goldberg on Owens' behalf.

2. Worst of enemies

RAW, **February 13, 2017:** Despite the tension between them, Jericho announced a "Festival of Friendship" that would celebrate his relationship with Owens. Jericho gave Owens a painting and a sculpture representing their friendship, but Owens was still mad at him. He attacked Jericho, leaving him badly injured. Days later, Jericho interfered in Owens' Universal Championship match against Goldberg, costing Owens the Title.

3. Walls come tumbling down

WrestleMania 33, **April 2, 2017:** After costing him the Universal Championship, Jericho challenged Owens to a match at *WrestleMania 33*. Owens accepted as long as Jericho put his United States Championship on the line. The match was an incredible display of personal animosity and in-ring skill. Jericho tried his Walls of Jericho move. Owens retaliated with his Pop-up Powerbomb slam, then pinned Jericho for the Championship.

"I am going to cause Chris Jericho's ultimate demise."

RAW, March 27, 2017

4. Bombed out

Payback, **April 30, 2017:** Jericho challenged Owens to a rematch at the next big event, *Payback*. Owens, who had started calling himself "The Face of America" after winning the United States Championship (despite being French-Canadian), agreed. Jericho pummeled Owens, who this time failed with his Pop-up Powerbomb. Jericho locked Owens in his Walls of Jericho submission hold and won the US Title.

5. Beyond personal

SmackDown, **May 2, 2017:** Owens claimed his automatic rematch opportunity two nights after *Payback* on *SmackDown*. The two fought ferociously, with Owens getting the victory and the United States Championship back. After the match, Owens continued to assault Jericho with a chair, injuring him badly. Jericho was taken from the ring on a stretcher, leaving WWE as a full-time Superstar.

THE NEW DAY
VS.
THE USOS

The Usos were considered one of the most experienced tag teams in WWE, having been multi-time Tag Team Champions during their decade as Superstars. While The New Day couldn't claim the same experience in WWE, they proved their skill and tenacity by keeping hold of the Tag Team Championship for 533 days, longer than any other tag team. Both teams strove to prove to the other that they were the better team.

DID YOU KNOW?

The New Day use the "Freebird Rule" to defend their Tag Team Championships. It means any two of the three members can defend the team's Titles at any time.

1. Tag team titles

Money in the Bank, June 18, 2017: The New Day were drafted to *SmackDown* and set their sights on SmackDown Tag Team Champions The Usos, who claimed to be invincible. The teams' first clash was at Money in the Bank. The Usos got themselves counted out by walking away from the ring and not returning within a 10 count. It meant The New Day won the match, but not the Championship.

2. New Day, new title

Battleground, July 23, 2017: The Usos again defended the Tag Team Championship against The New Day, though this time, the outcome was very different. New Day members Kofi Kingston and Xavier Woods both used their signature moves on Jimmy and Jey Uso to rattle them, before Woods pinned Jimmy to win the match and capture the Championship.

3. Re-rematch

SummerSlam, August 20, 2017: Big E and Xavier Woods represented The New Day in defending the *SmackDown* Tag Team Championship against The Usos. The Usos showed off their skills when they performed a massive double Samoan Splash off the top rope, smashing onto Big E, to win the match and regain the Titles.

4. Sin City showdown

SmackDown Live, September 12, 2017: The New Day had a chance to win back the Titles on *SmackDown* in Las Vegas in a Sin City Street Fight with no disqualifications or countouts. Both teams used chairs, tables, kendo sticks, and more in a bid to win. Kofi Kingston and Big E used their Midnight Hour move to grab the Tag Team Championship from The Usos once again.

RAP BATTLE

The New Day and The Usos had a rap battle filled with insulting barbs on the July 4, 2017 edition of *SmackDown Live*. The battle was judged by rapper Wale.

The New Day (Xavier Woods): Now, Jim. You and your brother, you're Tag Champs. You turned the Universe into believers. But please always remember you were absolutely nothing until your wife put you on *Total Divas*!

The Usos (Jimmy): The New Day and The Usos in a rap-off ... I was like, it can't be. What the hell they gonna talk about, Uce?

(Jey): I don't know, unicorns and stampedes!

"You talk about the 'power of positivity' but here's a dose of reality. For the last nine years we been here grinding, leaving blood, sweat, and tears in this ring."

—Jimmy, *SmackDown Live*, February 27, 2018

5. Hell in a tag team

Hell in a Cell, October 8, 2017: The two teams agreed to one more match, this time inside the first ever tag team Hell in a Cell Steel Cage Match. The match was intense, with both teams hitting hard. The Usos won back the Tag Team Championship by together flying off the top rope in their signature Samoan Splash, landing on and pinning Xavier Woods. But winning back the Titles has not ended the Usos' issues with The New Day. Their rivalry continues on.

AJ STYLES
VS.
SHINSUKE NAKAMURA

Shinsuke Nakamura and AJ Styles both refined their in-ring skills in Japan, mastering the art of hitting hard and striking fast in a form of combat known as "Strong Style." Nakamura and Styles used this method in many of their WWE matches, bruising and battering each other mercilessly as they tangled over the WWE Championship. It's a style unseen before in WWE, making thrilling matches for the WWE Universe.

5ft 11in (1.8m)

1. Pick your battles

WrestleMania 34, **April 8, 2018:** Shinsuke Nakamura won the 2018 Royal Rumble Match, earning his choice of Championship matches at *WrestleMania 34.* Nakamura picked AJ Styles and the WWE Championship. Their match at *WrestleMania 34* was a technical masterpiece with strong hits, holds, and counter-holds. Styles eked out a win and kept the Title, but had to absorb a sneaky low blow from Nakamura after the match.

2. Blow by low blow

Greatest Royal Rumble, **April 27, 2018:** In the weeks following *WrestleMania 34,* Nakamura repeatedly attacked Styles with low blows until a rematch for the WWE Title was signed for the historic *Greatest Royal Rumble* event—the first WWE event in Saudi Arabia. In their match, Nakamura again used low blows and other illegal tactics against Styles. It ended with the two Superstars fighting outside the ring too long, resulting in a double-countout draw.

6ft 2in
(1.87m)

3. No rules, no way out

Backlash, May 6, 2018: Just over a week after the *Greatest Royal Rumble*, Styles and Nakamura clashed at *Backlash*—this time in a no-disqualification match, where all blows and tactics were allowed. Styles used a chair on Nakamura, who replied with his usual low blow. The two Superstars then dealt each other simultaneous low blows, leaving both on the mat and unable to answer a 10 count. The result: yet another draw.

4. Winner fakes it all

SmackDown Live, May 15, 2018: With the issues between Nakamura and Styles continuing to escalate, *SmackDown* General Manager Paige set another match between them. The winner would pick the stipulation for their next scheduled match a month later at *Money in the Bank.* As usual, Styles and Nakamura fought ferociously. Nakamura pretended Styles had hit him with a low blow, faking intense pain. In the distraction that followed, Nakamura was able to hit Styles with his Running Knee Kinshasa move for the win.

RIVAL FACTS

- Styles is a two-time WWE Champion; Nakamura is a two-time NXT Champion.

- Styles and Nakamura have both won the United States Championship—Styles twice and Nakamura once.

- Nakamura won the 2018 Men's Royal Rumble Match; Styles has never won that 30-Superstar match.

5. Phenomenal display

Money in the Bank, June 17, 2018: As victor, Nakamura chose a Last Man Standing Match for his next match against Styles. The two foes exchanged many heavy hits. Styles hit one more low blow, then used his flying Phenomenal Forearm move on Nakamura, putting him through a table. Unable to answer a 10 count, Nakamura lost the match. Styles kept his Title and the prize of not having to face Nakamura for the Championship again.

Project Editor Pamela Afram
Senior Editor Alastair Dougall
Editors Beth Davies, Julia March, Rosie Peet
Senior Designer Nathan Martin
Project Art Editor Ray Bryant
Designer Anna Pond
Proofreader Kayla Dugger
Pre-Production Producer Marc Staples
Producer Lloyd Robertson
Managing Editor Paula Regan
Managing Art Editor Jo Connor
Art Director Lisa Lanzarini
Publisher Julie Ferris
Publishing Director Simon Beecroft

Global Publishing Manager Steve Pantaleo
Vice President, Consumer Products Sylvia Lee
Vice President—Photography Bradley Smith
Photo department Josh Tottenham, Frank Vitucci,
Georgiana Dallas, Jamie Nelson, Melissa Halladay, Mike Moran
Senior Vice President, Assistant General Counsel—Intellectual Property
Lauren Dienes-Middlen
Senior Vice President, Creative Services Stan Stanski
Creative Director John Jones
Project Manager Sara Vazquez

Dorling Kindersley would also like to thank Victoria Armstrong, Rosalyn Burton,
and Helen Murray at DK for editorial assistance

First American Edition, 2019
Published in the United States by DK Publishing
345 Hudson Street, New York, New York 10014

Page design copyright © 2019 Dorling Kindersley Limited
DK, a Division of Penguin Random House LLC
19 20 21 22 10 9 8 7 6 5 4 3 2 1
001–312643–Mar/2019

A catalog record for this book is available from the Library of Congress.

ISBN: 978-1-4654-8204-4

DK books are available at special discounts when purchased in bulk
for sales promotions, premiums, fund-raising, or educational use.
For details, contact: DK Publishing Special Markets
345 Hudson Street, New York, New York 10014
SpecialSales@dk.com

Photographs on pages 4–5, 6–7, 12–13, courtesy of Pro Wrestling Illustrated.

All other images © Dorling Kindersley
For further information see: www.dkimages.com

Printed and bound in China

A WORLD OF IDEAS:
SEE ALL THERE IS TO KNOW

www.dk.com
www.wwe.com